21 Mistakes Caregivers Make & How to Avoid Them

PRAISE FOR
21 Mistakes Caregivers Make & How to Avoid Them

Kudos to Toni Gitles, whose comprehensive guidebook, *21 Mistakes Caregivers Make & How to Avoid Them,* is a must-read! As the CEO of The Jewish Pavilion and the Orlando Senior Help Desk, I speak to caregivers every day of the week. Almost all of them are overwhelmed and have no idea where to start their inquiries. Toni's expert advice begins before care is needed while the person is cognizant and can discuss issues about future care. For example, she suggests that an adult child learns about and, if necessary, helps the elder organize their legal documents, medical information, and personal contacts.

As Toni eloquently describes in her book, for many adult children, there is a slow progression of tasks they assume as their parent ages. However, since these tasks may multiply at an alarming rate over time, I highly recommend that all adult children read *21 Mistakes Caregivers Make & How to Avoid Them* as soon as possible, take notes, and implement the solutions as needed. Toni emphasizes the importance of self-care, which includes knowing what you are dealing with and creating a supportive community.

Even with my experience working with seniors for over fifteen years, I found caregiving for my mother very stressful and challenging. I recommend Toni's suggestion that the caregiver gets help from family and friends and learns about available community resources, which made a world of difference for me. Toni's invaluable caregiving manual will change your life!

—**Nancy Ludin,** CEO of The Jewish Pavilion and the Orlando Senior Help Desk, Altamonte Springs, FL

Thanks for writing your book and being a consultant. Your comprehensive manual will save people a lot of time and heartache.
—**Jack Canfield,** Author and Speaker, Co-creator of the best-selling *Chicken Soup for the Soul*® series and Co-author of *The Success Principles*™

In her thoughtful book, Toni comforts us that we can rectify mistakes during our caregiving experience. She reminds us that our advocacy, tenacity, and caring hearts are the best ways we course correct.
—**Denise M. Brown,** Coach, Trainer, Author and Family Caregiver, Founder of The Caregiving Years Training Academy

Toni had both the burdens and the benefits of learning firsthand the challenges of caregiving. She showed strength and courage and then used this valuable life experience to provide insight and guidance to others traveling a similar journey. Her book, *21 Mistakes Caregivers Make & How to Avoid Them,* reflects her hard-won credentials to share her wealth of practical wisdom. As a seasoned estate planning and elder law attorney, I see the toll that caregiving takes on the caregiver. Now you can improve your caregiving experience with Toni's guidance on how to avoid common mistakes and misconceptions. Her straightforward, no-nonsense approach, with a dose of reality and humor, is a must-read for all caregivers.
—**Peggy R. Hoyt, J.D., M.B.A., B.C.S.,** Board Certified Specialist in Wills, Trusts, and Estates and Elder Law; Co-founder, The Law Offices of Hoyt & Bryan; Author of the Amazon Bestseller *101 Ways to F$$k Up Your Estate*

This is an important and much-needed book because many of us will become caregivers, likely when we least expect it. Toni Gitles has written a wonderful guidebook to help lessen anxiety and improve the confidence of those charged with the task. I will share this resource with my patients' caregivers.
—**Arnaldo Isa, MD,** Neurology Associates in Maitland FL

Toni Gitles' book is a cathartic journey down the path of caregiving. She gives voice and truth to the honor of caring for someone we love when the roles are reversed. It is a testament to a love story often untold and which we are totally unprepared for in life—the deepest measure of sharing life with another human being. I highly recommend this book to anyone serving the higher calling of caregiving.
—**Samantha Masterson,** CEO & President at Myasthenia Gravis Foundation of America, Inc.

The author brings a relational and relatable style to this caregiver tutorial. She has experienced all the points she discusses. The reader and caregiver will discover techniques and tips for making their caregiving experience manageable and rewarding.
—**Karen Cranmer-Briskey,** Former editor of an international hearing healthcare publication and experienced caregiver for her husband, who was 24 years her senior

I love the format. Very comprehensive. New caregivers often are very unprepared and don't know that they are. This book will be such an asset to those who find themselves as caregivers overnight as well as those who become caregivers gradually. I have already recognized some areas that we need to work on before we actually get to the point where one of us needs a full-time caregiver.
—**Helen Carter,** Professional caregiver

This book has an enormous amount of truly helpful information. It's brilliantly written and easy to find the information I needed. The action plan at the end of each Mistake was a wonderful way to create my personal care plan. It was like a roadmap that I could easily follow and get results.
—**Rebecca Minogue-Gitles,** Cared for her husband

Winston Churchill once said that if we fail to plan, we can plan on failing. Nothing in life is more important than your loved ones, and the statistics show that way more than likely, in your life, you will be wearing the hat of being a caregiver. Also, Benjamin Franklin said an ounce of prevention is worth a pound of cure. So, take Churchill's and Franklin's ideas here, and please pick up this book as Toni has put together a masterclass based on tried-and-true principles she learned while being a caregiver for her mother, May, for over a decade with zero regrets.

The result: 1. You will be ready if put on the caregiver path. 2. You will have zero regrets. 3. You will lessen your learning curve dramatically. But most importantly, you will discover something beautiful within yourself that few ever unlock. This book is beyond what you believe it is.

—**Much love, Jonathan Dunn,** Founder of The Dream Leader Institute

21 Mistakes is easy to read, understand and find the topics quickly that I most needed help with. The way the book is laid out makes it easy to use as a reference/resource, so you don't have to read the book all at once.

—**Susan Stern,** Cares for her mom, Founder, Spring to Life Coaching

I am very grateful that Toni Gitles has written *21 Mistakes Caregivers Make & How to Avoid Them,* which provides an exceptional reference guide with in-depth, informative descriptions, amazing insights, action plans, and stories that will benefit many current and future caregivers. Her expertise and dedicated talents to help others have been of direct benefit to me while working with me through my wife's dementia journey. In addition, Toni has been highly instructive in my role as a facilitator for a men's support group caring for loved ones with dementia. I am confident that all who read this book will improve their caregiving skills.

—**Dennis Dulniak, Ed.D.,** Caregiver, Care Partner, and Founder of Nana's Books Foundation and Central Florida Dementia-friendly Dining

As I delved into Toni's book, I was touched by how valuable it would have been if it had been available when my parents were nearing the end of their lives. I managed their Medical Directives-Living Power of Attorneys while working full-time and living nearby. Every chapter of the book contains a wealth of insightful information and recommendations. It allowed me to see the caregiving experience from both perspectives—as the caregiver and the one receiving care.

The chapter on love (Mistake # 21, Undervaluing Love in the Relationship) particularly resonated with me. It highlighted how I often had to handle challenging situations rather than spend quality time with my parents. Toni's perspective and recommendations are incredibly astute. Toni poured her heart and soul (along with all her vast knowledge and experience) into creating this invaluable reference resource. The information and concepts in this book should be taught in schools so that young people can learn how to support their grandparents and parents in practical ways and through sharing their love.

—**Lois Warnock,** Soul Divinity Healing & Art; Spiritual Coach – Strategist, Intuitive Artist

Toni Gitles has a unique "street smarts" approach to caregiving that will allow you to experience greater depths of compassion, hope, and joy. Buy her book now!

—**Steve Harrison,** Co-founder of www.AuthorSuccess.com

I am pleased to endorse Toni's book, *21 Mistakes Caregivers Make*. She has the personal insight from caring for her mother to give caregivers solid advice for dealing with their living situations. Toni has run our Caregivers' Support Group for the Myasthenia Gravis Foundation of America since 2021, and the group continues to grow. Her relaxed, practical attitude in the support group carries over to this book, which I recommend for all caregivers. She provides excellent tips to facilitate a healthy relationship between caregivers and their loved ones.

—**Dova Levin,** National Senior Director of Education and Patient Programming, Myasthenia Gravis Foundation of America, Inc.

Toni's book, *21 Mistakes Caregivers Make,* is the perfect roadmap to help you conquer any fears about caregiving. First, it's an easy-to-read, solution-filled guide to help ease your worries and answer questions while dealing with caregiving. Then, with tips and guidelines to navigate one of the most challenging chapters of your life, Toni helps you turn it into one of the most memorable. Yours in Health,
—**Tricia Lechmaier,** Owner and President, Lechmaier Family Chiropractic Center

Toni's book is akin to an encyclopedia covering many details necessary to know once you become a caregiver. Toni reveals to you most of the mistakes caregivers often make and how to make better choices. It is everything she learned through sheer trial and error, and she leaves no stone unturned.
—**Junie Swadron,** Author, *Your Life Matters!*

When I was thrown into managing my dad's estate after he died, it was a huge learning curve! I wasn't prepared at all to figure out where his Will was or what accounts he had open that I needed to close and who to notify. On top of that, to find out that my dad didn't even have an up-to-date Will when he died was costly and overwhelming. So, I especially value the chapter in Toni's book about organizing important papers for Power of Attorney and Executor for the Will. I wish I'd had more direction BEFORE I needed it! If you're caring for a parent or loved one now, you can't wait to get all the right paperwork in order, and even if that person is stubborn like my dad was, read this book now. You'll find a treasure of information, including action plans on what to do now versus later and how to navigate tough conversations. I wish I had had this information before my dad passed, and now that I am looking after my mom, who has lung cancer, I can ask more of the right questions, help her get everything in place sooner, and also enjoy this time with her more.
—**Katrina Sawa,** Business Coach for Entrepreneurs, Publisher, and 12x International Best-Selling Author with 20 books, including *Love Yourself Successful*

In *21 Mistakes Caregivers Make & How to Avoid Them*, Toni beautifully shares her personal caregiving story and intertwines the lessons learned as she inspires others to create meaningful moments with the family members in their care. Toni is open about the challenges and generously offers advice to help family caregivers find their path to a sustainable caregiving experience. Each chapter clearly defines a challenge caregivers face, explains why taking action is important, and then offers actionable steps to avoid common caregiving missteps. The final four chapters particularly touched me by demonstrating why staying connected with your purpose and reason for choosing to embark on this challenging journey is essential. Toni's wisdom and insights are practical and evoke all the emotions that arise when caring for a family member, allowing us to explore the growth opportunities that come with adversity. Thank you, Toni, for empowering caregivers with the confidence to navigate their journey!

—**Theresa Wilbanks,** Founder of Sustainable Caregiving, author of *Navigating the Caregiver River*, and Caregiving Consultant

"Nobody understands being a caregiver like another caregiver." In her book *21 Mistakes Caregivers Make & How to Avoid Them,* author Toni Gitles proves the truth of this statement. Giving examples from her caregiving experience with her mother, Toni takes us into the lonely yet loving world of family caregiving. Her "mistakes" allow others to learn and avoid some of the upset that is a natural part of caring for someone you love. After my work with family caregivers for over three decades, I can attest that even though all families are unique, many aspects of caregiving are predictably similar. Knowing where not to step is as important as knowing your options. I recommend this book by Ms. Gitles to families who care.

—**Mary Ellen Philbin,** CEO, Share the Care, Inc. www.helpforcaregivers.org

Caregivers frequently struggle to cope with the crisis of the moment. Stress levels rise to match the high stakes involved; we want to do right by those depending on us. Toni's *21 Mistakes that Caregivers Make & How to Avoid Them* provides clear paths to mental and logistical preparation, so each challenge doesn't feel like a crisis. The beauty and power of this book dwell in the personal stories Toni shares to guide us along the way. Caregiving can be overwhelming, isolating, and exhausting. Let this resource help you avoid regret, remorse, and the feeling of "I wish I had known earlier!" Let it be a treasured part of your support network that you turn to again and again. It's an understanding friend for you at 3 AM on a sleepless night. Let it be a source of comfort, reminding you that you can do this and you are not alone.

—**Gina Tyckoson,** Founder, ClarifySuccess.com
Certified Caregiving Consultant™ and Certified Caregiving Educator™
Certified Alzheimer's Disease and Dementia Care Practitioner™ and Certified Alzheimer's Disease and Dementia Care Trainer™

Congratulations to Toni for an amazing "Job well done" with her book, *21 Mistakes Caregivers Make & How to Avoid Them,* which touches my heart with reality and honest focus on the day-to-day struggles of caregiving.

Professionally, as an RN and CEO of Elite Cruises and Vacations, I create travel opportunities for caregivers and their loved ones with cognitive challenges. I focus on providing moments of JOY for our clients and life-long memories for their caregivers. As we strive to provide helpful education and practical takeaways for the caregivers, it frequently becomes painfully evident how demoralized and dispirited the caregivers are. Toni's book is the perfect reference and live-saving manual that most of us need.

Toni's masterpiece is an excellent roadmap for the difficult journey I am currently navigating, as my parents are in hospice. The factual information in my brain has drained out. As family caregivers, we must develop a spirit of self-care and mutual respect (even if our loved one does not participate).

Few of us were trained for family caregiving, so the emotional strain and overwhelming stress create an unexpected mess. Toni's book is an excellent assistant that puts us on a BETTER path with honest insights and action plans for daily functioning. The layout allows quick access to relevant information to assist with challenges we did not expect.

The learning curve for this caregiver gig is steep and challenging. With *21 Mistakes Caregivers Make & How to Avoid Them,* Toni has created a path to significantly reduce this challenge and help us move from crisis to SUCCESS.

—Kathryn M. Shoaf Speer, RN, BSN, ATP; owner and CEO Elite Cruises and Vacations LLC, Elite-Supported Travel/Dementia-Friendly Travel; Family Caregiver, Care Partner
www.EliteCruisesAndVacationsTravel.com

As a caregiver, I constantly sought help managing my mom's complex care needs. As her health worsened, my sense of overwhelm increased; I did not have the emotional bandwidth to read an entire book on caregiving. Several sit on my bookshelf today unread. What I love, love, love about *this book* is that by breaking down caregiving into 21 mistakes, the reader can go directly to the current problem or emotional trigger and grasp key aspects in just three or four pages. Checklists or action plans then get right to the steps so needed in the moment. Now that I am a professional caregiving partner, I will wholeheartedly recommend this book to my clients.

—Tanya Straker, Caregiver consultant and author of *6 Life Hacks for Family Caregivers: Be Your Own Coach & Beat Burnout*

21 Mistakes Caregivers Make & How to Avoid Them

Solutions and Strategies to Reduce Stress and Increase Happiness

Toni Claire Gitles, M.A.

Certified Caregiving Consultant™
Certified Caregiving Educator™
Certified Caregiving Facilitator™
Happy For No Reason Trainer

Goodyear, Arizona

Copyright © 2023 by Toni Gitles
21 Mistakes Caregivers Make & How to Avoid Them
First Edition

All rights reserved. No part of this book may be used or reproduced in any form by any means—digital photocopy, recording, or by electronic or mechanical means, including information storage and retrieval systems or Artificial Intelligence (AI) technology, without written permission from the author or the publisher, except for the use of brief quotations in a book review.

Printed in the United States of America

Paperback ISBN: 978-1-958405-99-4
Hardcover ISBN: 978-1-958405-88-8
eBook ISBN: 978-1-958405-89-5
Library of Congress Control Number: 2023911964

Publishing House: Spotlight Publishing House™ in Goodyear, AZ
https://spotlightpublishinghouse.com
Editor: Lynn Thompson, Living on Purpose Communications
Media Strategist and Design: Theresa Wilbanks, Sustainable Caregiving
Book Cover: Theresa Wilbanks and Dennis Dulniak
Interior Design: Marigold2k
Contact: Toni Gitles, CEO of Caregiver Empowerment, Heart Light Enterprises LLC. Toni@HOCToni.com
https://www. HOCToni.com or https://www.HeartOfCaregiving.com

Excerpts with permission from the author
The Caregiving Years, Your Guide to Navigating the Six Caregiving Stages by Denise M. Brown
Ninth Edition, Copyright © 2021
The Caregiving Years Training Academy and Denise M. Brown

Disclaimer

The information provided in this report should not be construed as legal, financial, or medical advice. Consult the appropriate professional for advice. You may not reproduce or distribute this report in any way. You may not sell it or reprint any part of it without written consent from the author, except for the inclusion of brief quotations in a review.

DEDICATION

1954 The Author

*To my mom and dad,
always my cheerleaders in life.*

May Campion Gitles   Emanual Gitles
1917-2017   1920-1989

*The love and sharing during my
fourteen-year caregiving experience with Mom
made it possible for me to share this wisdom with other caregivers.
Mom taught me that giving and receiving love
during adverse circumstances
is the journey and the joy.*

CONTENTS

Dedication xvii
Foreword xxiii
Preface xxvii
Introduction xxxi

PART I – UNPREPARED FOR A HEALTH CRISIS

Mistake # 1 Not Knowing Your New Title Is "Caregiver" 1

Mistake # 2 Not Having the Health Information You Need 9

Mistake # 3 Taking It All For Granted 17

PART II – EVERYTHING CHANGES AND YOU DON'T

Mistake # 4 Ignoring the Warning Signs 27

Mistake # 5 Denial: This Can't Be Happening 35

Mistake # 6 Deciding It Can Wait 45

PART III – YOU DON'T KNOW WHAT YOU DON'T KNOW

Mistake # 7 Not Shifting Your Mindset 55

Mistake # 8 Not Knowing Your New Responsibilities 65

Mistake # 9 Not Speaking Up To Authority 73

PART IV – YOU DON'T PRIORITIZE YOUR WELL-BEING

Mistake # 10 Failure To Put Your Oxygen Mask On First 81

Mistake # 11 You Don't Ask For Help 89

Mistake # 12 You Miss Out On Resources – Didn't Google It 97

PART V – INEFFECTIVE COMMUNICATION SKILLS

Mistake # 13 Not Knowing What Your Loved One Needs ...105

Mistake # 14 Not Finding Out How Others Can Help.......113

Mistake # 15 Settling For "Doctor-Speak" You Don't Understand 121

PART VI – NOT PLANNING FOR AN UNCERTAIN FUTURE

Mistake # 16 Not Having Legal Matters In Order 129

Mistake # 17 Not Assessing Financial Information.............135

PART VII – DISMISSING HAPPINESS

Mistake # 18 Not Celebrating With Your Loved One 145

Mistake # 19 Putting Your Happiness On Hold 153

Mistake # 20 Abandoning Your Religious Or Spiritual Practice 161

Mistake # 21 Undervaluing Love In The Relationship 167

Beyond Mistakes – Reflections 175

YOUR 21 SUPER POWERS FOR CAREGIVING 177

RESOURCES TO GET YOU STARTED 183

APPENDICES

1. In-Case-Of-Emergency Go Bag 187
2. Journaling 193
3. The Six Stages Of Caregiving 195
4. HIPAA 201
5. Action Plan For Building Your Care Community™........203

6.	Guidelines for Effective Conversations	209
7.	Preparation For A Doctor Visit	213
8.	Why You Don't Ask For Help	215
9.	Self-Care Action Plans	217
10.	Do Something Fun and Uplifting	225

Acknowledgments 229

About the Author 231

FOREWORD

When you meet someone for the first time, and they tell you that they are the primary caregiver for a loved one, do you think you have a good sense of what they do?

I thought I understood it well until I met Toni Gitles. In her book, she has shared what is truly involved in becoming a primary caregiver.

I then learned about the enormous responsibility it takes to manage the everyday details for a person who can no longer do these things for themselves. As a result, my respect for caregivers grew ever deeper. This book is for anyone navigating the caregiving experience who wants a better understanding of it.

In 2003, Toni's mother, May Gitles, was experiencing an unresolved health issue. Toni flew across the country from her home in California to Florida to take her mom to the doctor to get answers and a treatment plan. When the doctor failed to offer help for the problem ("Your mom's old, there's not much we can do"), Toni had one of those lightning bolt ah-ha moments. Her mom was not just getting old; she was 86! Since she could work remotely in her consulting position, Toni moved back to Florida, bought a home nearby, and prioritized spending time with her mom, helping her go through this stage in her life, and creating memories.

Listening to her intuition paid off when, in March 2006, Toni's mother, then 89 years old, was in the hospital when the doctor assessed her with a life-threatening illness. When told that her mom would never live independently again, Toni quickly surmised that she would now be the primary caregiver. Even though she was unsure about what that would entail, she was happy to be there to help and support her mom.

Toni imagined it might be a few years, at most, that her mom would need her, and she chose to do it willingly and lovingly as a privilege to be with her mom near the end of her life. However, nothing prepared her for what was coming—she would be her mom's primary caregiver for the next *eleven* years!

21 Mistakes Caregivers Make & How to Avoid Them is akin to an encyclopedia covering many essential details of preparing to be a caregiver and for those already caring for a loved one. Toni reveals most of the mistakes we can easily make and how not to make them. It is everything she learned through sheer trial and error, and she leaves few stones unturned.

Toni's practical guide is for what to do and what not to do from the first time you notice symptoms indicating your loved one's health is slipping or a medical professional tells you the person you love can no longer care for themselves.

While working with Toni as her book writing coach, I saw that this book is a masterpiece and is essential reading for every family member and professional caregiver. You will find confidence as you learn how to advocate for your loved one. Furthermore, this book belongs in every care home and every enrichment director's library. Finally, I am sure you will agree with me as you peruse and use the wisdom found in these pages that it would be glorious if every patient in every hospital received a copy of this book upon discharge.

I have worked with many authors over the years, and it is an absolute privilege to work with people who have the kind of integrity, passion, and dedication to their book as Toni. Her pure motivation in writing this book is to help others navigate this challenging terrain, so they don't need to operate in the dark as she did. Another aspect of this book that makes it a masterpiece is that it connects us to our common human experience. Every one of us will likely become a caregiver at some time in our lives, or we will be the recipient of such care. Toni shares her relatable personal stories—what she experienced emotionally throughout her caregiving years. Her words will comfort you and let you know you are not alone.

Toni also talks about how she felt later when she realized she was neglecting her own needs. She knew if she didn't attend to them, she would be incapable of caring for her mother or anyone else. Toni teaches you a new perspective on self-care and delivers her undeniable wisdom on every page. You will learn that this caregiving time in your life, although challenging, can also be a positive and life-affirming experience.

Imagine how it would be if you could bring a smile to your loved one's face whenever you walk in the room or they hear your voice. Don't be surprised to see this happen when you approach your loved one with an open heart, knowing that your energy carries an enormous impact. You can inspire enthusiasm and joy or, conversely, pain and fear. Let us all learn that every person deserves dignity, respect, and kindness.

Also, if you think there is nothing to look forward to since this may be the final stages of your loved one's life, it is not the case when you live fully in the present moment. Every moment offers the potential for magic to happen. So, learn to gather and collect wonderful memories now! Before long, this person may be gone from your life, so it is paramount to allow every moment to be an opportunity to discover little wonders and joys and make them matter. Not only will this improve the quality of life for the one you are caring for, but it will also offer you inspiration knowing there are still moments to savor. Although attention to important details can extend a person's life, perhaps love will give them a life of meaning, joy, peace, and comfort.

Toni also describes the delicate balance between allowing your loved one to express their opinion and make decisions about their care rather than predominantly making it for them. Instead, she invites you to support their position, make suggestions, and have a respectful conversation to identify their needs.

I find it astonishing how many aspects of caregiving there are and that Toni has covered so many of them, including resources that will guide you further.

If you are like me and like things to be relatively easy when needing help in a hurry, this book is your friend! You can look through the Table of Contents specifically for the area of caregiving relative to your needs and read what it says. In this way, each chapter stands alone. There are also bullet points and checklists that make reading quick, easy, and immediately understandable.

So, dear reader, if you suddenly need to assume the role of the primary caregiver for an aging parent, spouse, or someone else in your life and are looking for a way to handle it all, you can stop your search right now. You are holding the book that will answer many of your questions and those you haven't even considered.

I wish you ease and grace throughout this period with your loved one. May it be rich and meaningful and provide you with a sense of peace knowing you have given life-sustaining love and care during what is often the most delicate and profound time in a person's life.

God Bless You.
Junie Swadron, Author, Entrepreneur
www.junieswadron.com

PREFACE

"What do I do *now?*" I am standing next to the neurologist looking at a scan of Mom's brain when he informs me, "If your mom survives, she will never live independently again."

Mom was 89, and she did survive. After three weeks in rehab, I took her home and moved into her guest room. It was time to figure out what I was supposed to do now! No written instructions. No guidebook for caregiving. The hospital gave me the names of three rehab centers, and the only resource information rehab gave me was the name of the home health agency that would provide a nurse and occupational therapist to visit my mom weekly.

21 Mistakes Caregivers Make & How to Avoid Them is the book I needed at the time that I wish they had given me before we left the hospital to study before they released us into the wild unknown. It's a guide that would have reduced my stress and given me solutions and easy-to-implement tips to succeed at caregiving, creating memories, and enjoying the time Mom and I would have together until the end of her life.

As an only child, I knew the responsibility was all mine. My background in healthcare was helpful but didn't necessarily prepare me for all the caregiving responsibilities and decisions I would have to make. I began navigating our caregiving experience for the next eleven years with the expected nervousness of someone learning a new skill. I called on my knowledge from teaching at Baylor College of Medicine while I was on staff at several hospitals, learning how to communicate with physicians and training interns. Next, I mixed in trial and error, worked on patience, and let failure guide me. I learned from my mistakes, researched every new illness and treatment, and gleaned pertinent information, resources, and guidance from every healthcare professional we encountered.

After three months, when I realized I could no longer care for her in her home, I moved her into the nearby assisted living facility. Many staff there and at the hospital noticed me advocating for my mom and told me I was doing an exceptional job caring for her. I believed it too. It became my purpose in life to take care of Mom, entertain her, hire help for her, stay on top of her medical conditions, talk to doctors, and keep all her medications and medical history organized. I'm proud of that. Caregiving is hard, and I was a success. Well, mostly. Except for the part where you are supposed to "put your oxygen mask on first." I wore myself out trying to do everything perfectly. Uncertainty was always present. Since I'm not good with uncertainty, it added stress. There was always a new problem to solve. More specialty doctors kept getting added to my cell phone contacts. My learning curve was a steep climb.

The good news was I gained confidence with each successful outcome. The sad news was my stress, worry, and poor self-care exhausted me. If I had this book and someone who had been a caregiver who could walk with me on this uncharted journey, that would have been such a blessing.

My time teaching and working with physicians at Baylor College of Medicine proved extremely useful. I was an expert at asking them pertinent questions, although I found they were often in a hurry to examine Mom and leave. So, I often shouted to them as they walked out the door, "Wait, I have one more question!" Some were pleasant, while others hurried to get away. The important thing was I didn't give up advocating for mom.

I approach life with a positive attitude and a belief that everything happens for a reason, so I pay attention to the lessons, count the daily successes, and don't let the things that didn't work out, upset me. I applied the happiness principles of Positive Psychology (Science of Happiness) and sought regular comfort from our Maltese dog, Jasmine. My focus was on helping Mom achieve an exceptional quality of life regardless of circumstances. Being present in the moment, handling the things I could control, and not worrying about those I couldn't control, I celebrated my relationship with Mom for the time we had together, which turned out to be eleven years!

My very best wishes as you begin or continue your caregiving journey.

Treasure the moments with your loved one, practice giving and receiving love and kindness to all who cross your path, and deepen your relationships with family, friends, and professionals who support you and your loved one. May you become a partner in care so you end your experience with few regrets and treasured memories.

Toni Gitles
September 2023
Lake Mary, Florida

INTRODUCTION

It is a tragedy that most of us are untrained in caring for a family member. I agree with my friend, Tanya Straker, Certified Caregiving Consultant™ and former caregiver to her father, who believes that caregiving should be considered a life event like getting married, having children, establishing a career, and planning for retirement.

You are currently or will likely be a caregiver someday. You may also need care for yourself. Even if you have planned carefully and have siblings, the reality is that one person has the burden of caregiving, which can be overwhelming. While every person's situation is different, the combination of frustration, stress, worry, and a steep learning curve is common. Caregiving, whether short-term or long-term, interferes with work and family commitments and relationships, forces you to rearrange priorities and leisure time, may cause financial hardship, and can result in health issues and even death for *the caregiver*.

Over 53 million people in the United States are caregiving ("Caregiving in the U.S. 2020" by AARP and The National Alliance for Caregiving). Everyone needs to prepare for and learn about the caregiving journey so that when the crisis occurs, whether you or a family member, a loved one is prepared to step in and advocate, support, and bring essential information to the situation. There is no reason to see life as over; you can still be happy and celebrate.

WHAT'S IN THE BOOK?

This book gives you an understanding of the caregiving experience, your responsibilities, how to approach the challenges, be prepared for the stressors, and have a more joyful experience. My clients and current and former caregivers have reported these mistakes and solutions, and many I experienced while caring for my mother.

I use the word "Mistakes" instead of "Chapters" to bring your attention to the things that can blindside you if no one trained you to prepare for or notice them. To increase your confidence, I guide you in the skills to identify responsibilities, manage communication, and ask for support.

For example, as an only child, my parents raised me to be independent, to navigate the world on my own, and not rely on others. Well, there is some good advice and bad advice regarding caregiving. Caregiving is so much easier with people who help you. Alternatively, many can't do it alone without sacrificing their health, career, relationships, and financial well-being.

Part I: Unprepared for a health crisis. You don't relate to the title "Caregiver," you don't organize the health history of your loved one (or yourself), and you take your responsibilities for granted.

Part II: Everything changes, and you don't. You may notice warning signs but ignore them. There may be denial thinking, for example: "This can't be happening," and deciding that taking action to help your loved one can wait.

Part III: You don't know what you don't know about caregiving because you haven't been there before. As a result, you fail to shift your mindset about the circumstances and your role. Therefore, you are unaware of your new responsibilities and don't speak up to authority.

Part IV: You don't prioritize your well-being. You don't take care of yourself first, ask for help, or look for and find resources to support you and your loved one.

Part V: Ineffective communication skills with your loved one, family, and physician. You fail to find out what your loved one needs and wants and how family and friends can help, and you settle for an incomplete understanding of doctor's orders and explanations.

Part VI: Not planning for an uncertain future, you don't have legal documents in order and are unaware of financial information for yourself or your loved one.

Part VII: Dismissing happiness and celebrating life because of the health issue or deterioration, and you put your permission to enjoy living on hold and cease or question your connection and guidance with a higher power. Not realizing when you undervalue giving and receiving love in your relationships.

WHY DO I FOCUS ON MISTAKES?

For a long time, I didn't realize that there are often mistakes and failures on the road to success. I was well into adulthood when I realized mistakes could teach us a lot—they help us course correct. They are part of our journey as humans, and when we learn from our mistakes, we use that knowledge to make better choices next time, be more effective at the task, and grow. So while making a mistake is disheartening, I've come to terms with what it means to do my best and make the best decision based on current information and wisdom. In other words, while it can still be frustrating, it's no longer a source of stress.

Having a heads-up on mistakes caregivers make can be helpful but does not guarantee that you will be able to avoid them. What's important is having a guide to identify mistakes and provide solutions that will help decrease stress, increase confidence, and get you on a manageable path.

HOW TO READ THIS BOOK?

Each part is a focus for a set of related mistakes. Each mistake is an independent unit, so feel free to read them in any order and read the ones first that apply to your current situations and needs.

I designed the format to be easy to read so you can quickly find the specific information you need. Please write in the book, highlight relevant sections, and tag pages with sticky notes. By completing the action plan exercises at the end of each chapter, you will create a dynamic caregiving plan you can implement, which will relieve stress, and some uncertainty. Put yourself in control of the things you actually *can* control. In caregiving, as in life, things don't always go as planned. Your reaction and attitude influence your experience.

Each mistake has the same format. I begin with an introduction and a story followed by highlights of why the mistake is important and why it may be difficult to implement the solution. The action plan is next, which may be a checklist or step-by-step approach. You personalize the information here by answering questions and creating your caregiver action plan.

I've created an official companion workbook with all of the action plans and appendices to make it easy for you to create your personalized action plan and have it all in one place.

WHAT MORE CAN YOU DO AS A CAREGIVER?

Consider joining a support group. Put your self-care first so you can be at your best. Follow your intuition and keep an open communication channel with your loved one and everyone involved in their care. Find an inspirational quote and put it in a place you will see it every day to remind yourself how every moment of your life is exceptional and deserves your full attention. By focusing on the present moment and treating every action and every person with respect, you may find a new relationship with life and a renewed reason to celebrate life and find happiness despite your circumstances.

My suggestion for you is that it is time to stop thinking:

- I do not need to know this information yet

- My family is all healthy right now, and I can't imagine becoming a caregiver or needing one soon

- If something happens to my parents, someone will take care of them

- This does not affect me because there is no history of dementia, Alzheimer's, or cancer in my family

- I will wait until there is a crisis, and then I'll just figure it out

It is time to learn about and reflect on the *21 Mistakes that Caregivers Make & How to Avoid Them.* Let's get started.

A GENTLE CAUTION

Caring for a parent, spouse, or family member may be the most difficult thing you do. The information in this book may be overwhelming at first. It was not my intention to overwhelm you or make life more complicated. On the contrary, by accepting your circumstances, keeping a positive mindset, asking for help, taking one day at a time, and following the suggestions in this book, you can experience greater ease, less overwhelm and stress, and increased confidence and happiness in your caregiving journey. Be open to receiving the help and support I offer in this book.

It is truly a gift from my heart to yours that you may experience as much love and happiness in your life as you allow in.

*All of us in our lives are going to suffer difficult times.
And the question is: Can you get through it?
Can you grow through it? Can you learn from it?
And then those adversities become learning experiences.*
—Doris Kearns Goodwin
American biographer, historian, political commentator

PART I

UNPREPARED FOR A HEALTH CRISIS

*One day you will tell your story of how you overcame
what you went through and it will be
someone else's survival guide.*
—Brené Brown
American research professor, lecturer, author, podcast host

The Rosalynn Carter Institute for Caregivers (RCI) was established in 1987, rooted in former First Lady Rosalynn Carter's belief that there are only four types of people in the world: Those who have been caregivers, those who are caregivers, those who will be caregivers, and those who will need a caregiver.

www.rosalynncarter.org

MISTAKE # 1

NOT KNOWING YOUR NEW TITLE IS "CAREGIVER"

You may recently have become aware that a family member could use help due to aging or a health issue, or you may currently be in the throes of caring for a loved one. Chances are you see yourself as a daughter or son taking care of a parent, spouse, or partner, caring for your significant other, or caring for another family member. In many cultures, it is tradition or an expected role we take on, and it doesn't come with the label "caregiver."

Even when providing extensive care, the word "caregiver" does not initially exist in your vocabulary. However, as the time spent caring for this person and your responsibilities increase, you realize your life has a new normal, and your primary focus is *giving care* to your loved one.

Suppose you care for an individual with a chronic illness or multiple health conditions. In that case, your life changes dramatically, and perhaps because of the daily or even 24/7 care you deliver, you may have an ah-ha moment when you self-identify as a "caregiver."

Consider that all people are prospective caregivers. People are living longer and getting short-term, chronic, and life-threatening diagnoses. You will likely care for someone or several people throughout your lifetime and possibly need a caregiver yourself. It is the way the world works today. Therefore, normalizing the word "caregiver" and giving it a positive connotation is of great value.

Mom wakes up one morning in pain and unable to walk. She calls me using the bedside telephone and, in a stressed voice, tells me she needs help to get out of bed. I drive right over to see what is wrong.

I am startled and frightened to see Mom lying in bed, helpless and crying for me to help her. My first thought is, "How am I even going to be able to get her to the bathroom?" Her need is urgent! Yesterday, Mom was strong and healthy. Today, at 89, she suddenly looks delicate and frail. Once I help her out of bed, holding on to Mom securely to make sure she doesn't fall, I am relieved to notice she does have some strength to put one foot in front of the other to get to the toilet. Once she completes that essential task, I help her dress in loose, comfortable clothes and grab her "In-Case-of-Emergency" Go Bag (See Appendix 1 for ICE) as I help her walk to my car. Once I get her buckled into the front seat, we head to the Central Florida Regional Hospital Emergency Department in Sanford, Florida, as quickly as possible. It is a terrifying 25-minute drive. I'm constantly asking Mom, "You okay?" I later learned that since I could not assess her symptoms, it would have been much wiser to call for an ambulance and follow it to the hospital. Fortunately, we arrive without her condition worsening. Lesson noted for the future.

The admissions person immediately recognizes the crisis Mom is experiencing. She facilitates our admission to get vitals taken and a room assigned. It is an exhausting day: a history taken, a physician visit, tests, and a no-doubt-about-it-something-is-terribly-wrong admission with a diagnosis of infection of unknown origin. Followed by an even more exhausting, three-week hospital stay when the neurologist tells me to "prepare for the worst, and, if she does survive, she will never live independently again."

The doctors are shocked. Mom survives and after three weeks in rehabilitation, I can take her home. But, just as the doctor said, she cannot live independently. So, because I feel like I have no choice, I temporarily move in to take care of her and assess the situation.

I cared for my mother for three years before identifying with the term caregiver. Since the word had never been in my vocabulary, it didn't occur to me to refer to myself as one. The delay in recognizing my role and a new identity as a "caregiver" was unfortunate since earlier awareness would have helped me navigate my journey. I might have learned it's acceptable and even necessary to ask for help, identify those individuals who could support me, and be more organized in finding companies that I could hire for help.

What I did feel initially and often throughout the caregiving years was that I was an overwhelmed, dutiful daughter, worried and wondering what I would face on a day-to-day basis. Would I be able to leave Mom alone? What help should I ask for or services should I request, and could we afford this situation financially? How does an only child manage this new reality, and what will the future hold?

Let's explore why it is important to identify as a caregiver, why it may be difficult, and the steps you can take to embrace your caregiver identity.

Why Identifying As A Caregiver Is Important

- ♥ Caregiver is the common term used in the United States to describe someone helping or caring for another individual. When you connect with this term that signifies you are caring for another human and likely for someone you truly love and care about, you will begin to look for and receive support for your work as an unpaid caregiver.

- ♥ Caregiving is lonely, which can lead to overwhelming sadness and depression. When you identify with the caregiver title, you join the estimated 53 million people in the greater national caregiving community. As a part of the ever-growing, extensive caregiving community, you can participate in that community and reap the benefits of lessons learned from other caregivers, educational programs, and respite opportunities.

- ♥ You will find resources in your community, nationally, and online that can support you and help you in your caregiver role, services that can be beneficial in reducing stress and decreasing unmet needs for both you and your loved one. Resources in rural areas are likely limited. Do your best to locate national and online information and support.

- ♥ You can't anticipate all that you will need. However, your connection to resources and fellow caregivers will help you better predict where your caregiving path will lead. As your network grows, you connect with online and in-person support groups, social media groups, national, regional, and local organizations, consultants, authors, podcasters, and other businesses to provide resources and services specifically for caregivers.

- ♥ When you identify as a caregiver, you recognize your role as your family member's care advocate. You gain increased confidence when talking to healthcare professionals about your loved one's care. You enjoy a sense of fulfillment, purpose, and satisfaction.

♥ **Why is identifying as a caregiver important to you?**

Why Identifying As A Caregiver May Be Difficult

- The word "caregiver" may not be in your vocabulary.

- If you believe the word "caregiver" has a negative connotation, you may not refer to yourself as a caregiver. Or, you may have a preconceived idea of what a caregiver "looks like," and you do not fit that image.

- **Why is identifying as a caregiver difficult for you?**

ACTION PLAN: Identify As A Caregiver

Understand and accept your new identity as a caregiver and use the word to empower you in your new role. You are not "just" a daughter, spouse, cousin, or family member. You are the individual who cares about this person or your loved one, and they may rely on you to be their advocate in many circumstances. You are a caregiver!

1. Continue to read this book thoroughly. Access the available information and resources to save time and money, reduce stress, and for education and solutions to your caregiving challenges.

2. Identify the tasks you do for your loved one and notice how much time you spend on each task while caring for them. (See Part III, Mistake # 8)

    a. Food shopping

    b. Food preparation, cooking, and clean-up

    c. Provide transportation

    d. Run or assist with errands

    e. Health monitoring

    f. Emotional support

    g. Discuss and document medical history, medications, hospitalizations, COVID-19 and other vaccine information

    h. Document physician contact information

    i. Assist with personal care: bathing, dressing, grooming, feeding, mobility

    j. Hire home companion help

    k. Other

3. Begin to identify the help you may need to take care of your loved one. What tasks can you delegate? Who could help with those tasks?

4. How do you feel about your caregiving role and the responsibilities? Begin to identify what *you* need to do to maintain your mental, physical, emotional, and spiritual health. (See Part IV, Mistakes # 10, 11, 12)

5. How has caregiving affected your other responsibilities?

    a. Work

    b. Family

    c. Recreation/Leisure

    d. Travel

    e. Other

6. Identify the support available in your community and nationally for caregivers. (See Resources) Seek the expertise of a Certified Caregiving Consultant™ who understands what you are going through and can provide guidance and numerous forms of assistance.

7. What can you do now to access and use the resources that you need or will need in the future?

8. Journal your thoughts and feelings daily. The more you get to know yourself in the role of caregiver, the more empowered you will become. (See Appendix 2)

Please visit www.HOCToni.com/actionplan/
for a free download of this Action Plan.

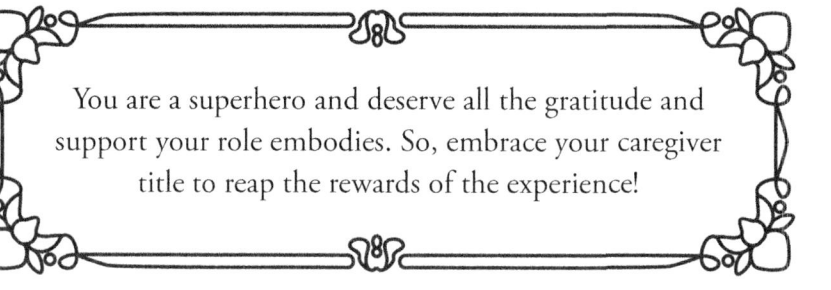

> You are a superhero and deserve all the gratitude and support your role embodies. So, embrace your caregiver title to reap the rewards of the experience!

For many people, illness – loss of health – represents the crisis situation that triggers an awakening. With serious illness comes awareness of your own mortality, the greatest loss of all.
—Eckhart Tolle, German-born spiritual leader and self-help author

MISTAKE # 2

NOT HAVING THE HEALTH INFORMATION YOU NEED

You may think, "When they need me, I will be there." You are a great daughter, son, spouse, partner, for recognizing a loved one may need care someday and deciding that you will be available for them! Every individual needs the emotional support only you can provide.

Especially if you are not currently caring for someone, it's time to consider yourself an "Expectant Caregiver," one of the terms suggested by Denise M. Brown in her explanation of *The Caregiving Years, Your Guide to Navigating the Six Caregiving Stages,* Ninth Edition, Copyright © 2021 (as paraphrased here; see Appendix 3 for the full excerpts).

In Stage 1, *The Expectant Caregiver,* you consider that there is likely someone in your life that may need care sometime in the future, possibly soon, since a crisis often occurs unexpectedly. Therefore, preparation and planning are essential whether you are a caregiver now or expect to be one.

If you currently care for someone and are reading this book, you are likely in one of the following stages:

Stage 2 – *The Freshman Caregiver*
You've begun to help your family member regularly, weekly, perhaps even a few times a week. Your duties range from errand-running and bill-paying to some assistance with hands-on care.

Stage 3 – *The Entrenched Caregiver*
Your involvement with your loved one is almost daily, if not constant. You may live together (in your home or theirs), or your involvement means you structure your day to be available to them.

Stage 4 – *The Pragmatic Caregiver*
You have been helping a family member or friend for a long time. You've been through it all: hospital admission and discharges, short-term rehab stays in nursing homes and a vast array of community services. You have a practical, realistic approach toward your caregiving role, and you would have given up a long time ago without your sense of humor—a critical tool for your survival.

See Appendix 3 for a thorough description of all six stages.

In Mistake #1, I talked about the sudden health crisis with my mother. Due to her age, we had long prepared for a possible emergency.

When you show up at a hospital emergency department to support your loved one, it is valuable for their emotional well-being, whether they've been in a car accident or had a sudden personal health crisis. You also want to support their physical well-being. Knowing and providing your family member's medical information, including a list of medications and allergies, is crucial. As your family member's care advocate, the hospital staff will need this information to treat your loved one effectively.

"What, I need to prepare?" you might ask. "Nobody ever told me that."

You are not alone. Nobody ever told most of us. This mistake, not having the medical information you need, can result from not identifying as a caregiver, Mistake # 1.

When you underestimate your caregiver role and responsibilities, you are ill-prepared to advocate for a family member during a crisis. Your knowledge of your loved one's medical information is critical in a short-term care crisis or a long-term caregiving experience.

At 56, I desire to know as much as possible to assist in Mom's care or manage it effectively. So, as I accumulate new information at each doctor appointment, I add it to the notebook. Fortunately, she welcomes me knowing all this information.

For example, an unplanned crisis occurs in the emergency department when Mom and I are still there at 11 pm waiting for the physician, and it's time for her bedtime medication. I have her medication list with me and ask the staff to administer one of the drugs that will make Mom more comfortable. They have limited access to the pharmacy, and one staff member comes back and tells me they'll give her a substitute medication, which concerns me. Mom immediately has a severe reaction, so instead of going home soon, we have a change of plans, they admit Mom to the hospital for observation. After that episode, I always carry Mom's scheduled medications and Tylenol because she often experiences pain.

Remember that despite your presence at the hospital emergency department or doctor's office with your loved one's (or your own) accurate medical information does not guarantee the successful transfer of this information to a medical file. Scanning documents decreases the likelihood of errors. However, hospitals may still use manual data entry, and it is helpful to be there to oversee every aspect of care. Verify information when possible. Get accustomed to using patient portals on healthcare websites to access medical notes and test results and communicate with your physicians.

Let's explore why gathering health information is important, why it may be difficult, and how to begin the process of collecting your loved one's vital health information.

Why Having Health Information Is Important

- ♥ Preparing for a hospitalization by gathering medical information relieves the stress that comes with a crisis.

- ♥ Preparation enables you to be organized, bring critical information at a moment's notice, and advocate, saving you time and improving care outcomes.

- ♥ During a visit to the Emergency Department (ED), troubleshooting and diagnosis are more efficient when you provide health history and details to the medical team.

- ♥ At the ED, the absence of a driver's license, ID card, or insurance information can be a distressing distraction when you are concerned about your family member's health status.

- ♥ Hospital staff requires emergency contact and surrogate healthcare information, and without it, the patient is left alone without an advocate at a critical time.

- ♥ **Why is having health information important to you?**

Why Having Health Information May Be Difficult

- You don't know what you don't know and planning for the "what if?" situations can be overwhelming. I emphasized this need for preparation in my chapter, "Jumpstart Your Caregiving Skills," in the compilation book *Jumpstart Your… Vol III (2020)*. A crisis, health-related or accidental, can happen quickly and unexpectedly.

- Family members, especially parents or relatives, may be reluctant to discuss their medical condition. It is a sensitive topic because the request for details may be perceived as too personal and invasive, making it an uncomfortable conversation.

- **Why is having health information difficult for you?**

ACTION PLAN: Gather and Organize Health Information Now

Today is the best time to get started. There is no time to search for or gather this information in an emergency. Therefore, time is of the essence. Start a conversation to relieve *STRESS* before a crisis to ensure essential health information is ready for the on-site healthcare team.

"I thought we should do some planning. In case of a medical emergency, I want to be there for you, so you receive the best support possible. It would give me peace of mind if we could talk about your health issues and medications."

1. Schedule time with your loved one to ask questions and gather information.

2. Check your state's designation for Health Care Surrogate or Medical Power of Attorney, the individual named in a legal document to make health care decisions if the loved one cannot make them. Ask who your loved one has assigned this power. It may or may not be you, or they may not have named one in their legal documents. If they haven't established a proxy, encourage your loved one to work with an eldercare attorney to name a Health Care Surrogate or Medical Power of Attorney. Critical! Make this a #1 priority.

3. The Health Insurance Portability and Accountability Act of 1996 (HIPAA) is a federal law requiring the creation of national standards to protect sensitive patient health information from being disclosed without the patient's consent or knowledge. Have your loved one add you to their HIPPA-approved list for access to their healthcare information. See HIPPA regulations. (See Appendix 4)

4. Prepare an "In-Case-Of-Emergency" Go Bag (ICE), notebook, and plan. (See Appendix 1) In the case of loved ones unable to gather this information, a trusted family member or caregiver can help. This notebook of medical information will include at minimum:

    a. Your loved one's name, date of birth, address, phone, and email. Your name and contact information, including for other family members.

    b. Contact information for primary and specialized physicians, health care providers, and pharmacy.

    c. A comprehensive word document noting medications (include the name, dose, when taken and why, and doctor who ordered it), allergies, and medical history, including dates of COVID-19 and other vaccinations, hospitalizations, and surgeries.

    d. Copies of your loved one's driver's license (or State ID card), health insurance information, Health Care Surrogate legal documents, and Do-Not-Resuscitate Orders (DNR).

5. You may need to go through a pile of unorganized paperwork to find what you need and create lists and spreadsheets to organize the information.

6. Decide how you will organize information: a 3-ring binder with sections, a folder, a healthcare or caregiver app, shared

google drive, information on your cell phone, computer files, or a system you develop. I recommend a hard-copy system as it provides quick access for sharing with health care professionals who often scan the information into a computer. You can also post it in a hospital room or anywhere a professional caregiver might work with your loved one.

7. Print at least three updated copies of the medical information spreadsheet for doctor appointments and health care providers to transfer information to relevant persons quickly. Update and reprint copies as medication or health history changes.

8. Order medical alert bracelets for older family members with critical health issues (e.g., heart attacks, neurological disease, any form of dementia, cancer), which includes their condition and family contact information, always accessible.

Suggestion: Document this medical information for yourself, with your children, spouse, or care partner, and parents, ESPECIALLY if there is a family history or previous history of a debilitating illness.

Please visit: www.HOCToni.com/actionplan/
for a free download of this Action Plan.

Your caregiver CEO skills will serve you, your loved one, and the health care team well during a medical emergency and routine doctor's visits. Enjoy the confidence of being prepared when you present organized documents that will help the medical team expedite exceptional care.

*It's the human desire in all of us
to want to make life better for somebody else.
It makes you feel larger.
It makes you feel part of the whole human race.
And if you can make that transition in even a small way,
and then it becomes larger and larger,
it's something that deepens you as a person.
It's a much better source of ambition than just for self.*
—Doris Kearns Goodwin
American biographer, historian, political commentator

MISTAKE # 3

TAKING IT ALL FOR GRANTED

How do you feel about your caregiver role? Resentful? Anxious? Terrified? Or perhaps Comfortable? Grateful? Prepared? Each of these responses is valid. You might be asking many questions: Why me? Why now? How do I fit more responsibility into my life? Do I want this in my life? Do I have a choice? What does it mean to give care to this person?

Perhaps being a caregiver isn't something you are choosing. You might think your life will no longer be in your control, it's not fair, or how do I get out of this? Since we are humans used to reacting to circumstances, these thoughts are not unusual.

While no one is happy when a loved one's health fails and you are called on to provide care, accepting and welcoming the opportunity is possible when you recognize that caring for your family member gives your life meaning. You can view caregiving as a way to fulfill your purpose, express love, learn, and grow. Growth comes from adversity, and while you don't know what challenges you will face, you can choose to accept the struggles and have faith that you have the strength required to survive and even thrive.

There are no rights or wrongs here. Notice your reaction and your thoughts. Why not approach your new circumstances with enthusiasm, passion, presence, and purpose? The care you provide for another human is no small feat and should be respected and treated with loving kindness.

At the beginning of caring for Mom, I had no idea how this journey would change my life for the positive. I am grateful to have resolved any anger and resentment early on so that I would never take this experience for granted. Instead, I could consider it an opportunity for growth and experiencing love and happiness in a completely new way.

My dad died suddenly in 1989. Mom was devastated, and her grief was overwhelming. After a period, she gathered the strength every day to continue going to work in our business, but once home, she cried all night. This routine went on for nearly a year. At some point, when she felt willing and able to talk with me, she asked me to promise that if she ever needed help because of aging or a health issue, I would be there for her. As an only child, I could've felt obligated or angry at her request, but it was an easy promise to make. It wasn't until 2003 that I realized Mom needed some assistance. The health crisis that solidified my title as a caregiver began in 2006.

I immediately understood this would be a complex project and considered how best to get organized for what I never expected to be such a long journey.

In a journal, I wrote guidelines or intentions, as they are referred to today, to keep me grounded and focused. It was a short document I would refer to often over the years.

> First, I will provide Mom with the best medical care possible so she has the best quality of life. If she feels up to it, I will ask, "What activities or outings could we take that would be fun and create a memory?" Secondly, to will have no regrets when Mom dies. That means evaluating every action,

decision, health event, and doctor visit. Also, being present to the circumstances, Mom's wishes, and what feels like the right actions. Third, to never take this time with my mother for granted. Yes, putting so much attention on one person for so many years is challenging. But it becomes more manageable when I realize that the one person is my mom, who loves me more than anything in the world and treats me with love and kindness every day. And it is the most precious thing in the world to know, love, and understand my mom and her life journey.

*Let's explore why
taking nothing for granted is important,
why it may be difficult,
and how you can cherish every moment.*

Why Taking Nothing For Granted (Cherishing The Journey) Is Important

- ♥ You know that caring for a loved one gives your life meaning and purpose. Caregiving or helping other caregivers may emerge as a calling you were unaware of, inspiring you to write a book or a blog about your journey.

- ♥ You find strengths you did not know you had. It changes you positively in many ways, and you approach the future with an open mind. When you reflect on your caregiving experience with your loved one, your perspective of this time will be different than it is today, a year, two years, or five years, after your loved one passes.

- ♥ You can look back with few regrets and appreciate how your decision to embrace the caregiving role created a meaningful journey as a gift for you and this person.

- ♥ The alternative could be a less fulfilling life focused on being the victim, blaming others, struggling, and stressing about your circumstances that will rob you of happiness.

- ♥ When you engage fully in life, with as much joy and enthusiasm as you can muster, you can create unexpected positive experiences. You may discover lovely surprises about your loved one—learning something fascinating and new. You may have conversations with other caregivers that bond you together for life. You may receive advice that has made your life simpler and develop a new relationship with your religion or spirituality. You may find an intimacy with your loved one that you didn't know could exist.

- ♥ **Why is cherishing every moment important to you?**

Why Taking Nothing For Granted (Cherishing The Journey) May Be Difficult

- Your feelings can overwhelm you. Be honest about your initial feelings, thoughts, and actions related to being a caregiver.

- Being the primary caregiver can be lonely. Accept and forgive when family and friends can't or won't share or avoid caregiving responsibilities.

- You may have to manage a career, family, and caregiving, constantly assessing how to balance everything on your plate.

- Your inexperience can be unsettling. Settle in, gather as much information as possible about caregiving, and address the duties of a part-time or full-time caregiver.

- Burden or blessing? Acknowledge the possibility that caring for a loved one may be the greatest gift you receive in your life, even if you don't believe it now, as many don't at the beginning of their journey.

- **Why is cherishing the journey difficult for you?**

ACTION PLAN: Taking Nothing For Granted (Cherishing The Journey)

Work through the action plans offered throughout the book. Focusing on solutions will help you feel more in control.

1. Journal your caregiving experience. Write daily gratitudes. Document events. Write about the feelings that made you light up and feel good. Write your successes daily. Review your entries at the end of every month to get a profound sense of your experience.

2. Keep track of the meaningful moments and celebrations with your loved one each day, week, and month.

3. Which family and friends can you invite into your caregiving journey, and how can you celebrate life?

4. What lessons about life has your caregiving experience taught you so far?

5. What strengths have you discovered in yourself because of caregiving?

6. How do you find the strength and motivation to continue caregiving every day?

7. How are you taking care of yourself with regular breaks?

8. Take photos and videos of and with your loved ones, family, and friends, to enjoy with your loved ones and others later.

9. Connect with other caregivers to learn what they consider the "gifts" they receive from caregiving.

10. Early on, invite family and friends to spend time with you and your loved one, sharing the experience without asking them for specific help that they might refuse, creating a distance between you. (See Part IV, Mistake # 11, and Part V, Mistake # 14)

11. Explore your thoughts and reservations. Are you doubtful that caregiving is a gift to be cherished? Try harder and be patient. It may hit you much later.

Please visit www.HOCToni.com/actionplan/
for a free download of this Action Plan.

> Keep reading! You are on a meaningful journey. Take the opportunity to collect beautiful souvenirs. Take photos and videos and fill a scrapbook with notes and mementos to capture the loving, meaningful, and fun moments that will become your favorite memories.

PART II

EVERYTHING CHANGES AND YOU DON'T

So often in life, things that you regard as an impediment, turn out to be great good fortune.
—Ruth Bader Ginsburg, American lawyer, and jurist, Associate Justice of the Supreme Court of the United States, from 1993 until her death in 2020

Have a firm embrace of reality. Just because it's bad doesn't mean it will always be bad. Just because its challenging right now, doesn't mean that it will always be challenging.
—Michael Balchan, Head Coach + Chief of Staff of Heroic, Public Benefit Corporation

MISTAKE # 4
IGNORING THE WARNING SIGNS

The more time you spend with your loved one, the less likely you will notice small changes in behavior and routines that, while they don't seem right, appear inconsequential in the context of daily living. At some point, however, the small changes become more evident, which frequently happens with people who are eventually diagnosed with mild cognitive impairment (MCI) and, often later, some form of dementia.

A change in a family member's abilities may be more noticeable if you see them infrequently, perhaps at birthday celebrations or the holidays. You might notice things out of place or clutter accumulating in their home. It can be a shock to suddenly realize that your family member's abilities or behaviors have changed or are not what you remembered. The typical response initially is, "Now, what do I do?" The realization that you don't know what to do can be unsettling.

It is important to rely on instinct and continue searching for solutions when you suspect more is happening beneath the surface. You are, after all, usually more familiar with your loved one than most people. You can look to professionals for answers but may not always find the right person who can support you. Certified Caregiving Consultant™, Senior advisors or Senior Care Managers might best assist.

As an example of something not quite right, my friend's mother repeatedly got lost while driving to places that were previously routine destinations. Sometimes she found the destination and other times continued to drive around until she found her way back home.

In another instance, when I met her mother for lunch, I referred to the last time we ate at the restaurant where we were, and what we ordered from the menu, and she said she didn't remember being together just weeks before. Both these situations were red flags.

My friend noticed the problem immediately and indicated a growing number of disturbing situations. When my friend took her mother to the next doctor's appointment, she mentioned all the concerns and that she was worried that her mom might be in the early stage of dementia. The primary physician conducted a brief screening test and determined everything was fine. That was it, except her mom felt she won a victory, and arguments continued as the daughter kept pointing out behavior and memory issues while her mom argued that nothing was wrong. Frustration and upset increased for both parties.

The family started documenting their mom's medical history, accompanied her to doctor visits, and eventually took away the car keys. They also sought advice from a financial planner and elder care attorney to prepare for future medical costs and documented their mom's wishes.

A year later, a different approach included an evaluation by a neurologist in a clinical trial setting, and they enrolled her mom in the trial. Further testing resulted in a diagnosis of Alzheimer's.

In this case, the family did not ignore the warning signs. However, because there was no support from the family physician, they felt they had run out of options to address the behavior and get cooperation from their mom. Thankfully, they made important preparations for the future while they could still include their mom in the decisions affecting her.

*Let's explore why paying attention
to the warning signs is important,
why it may be difficult,
and how you can reduce uncertainty.*

Why Paying Attention To The Warning Signs Is Important

- ♥ Your life is full of circumstances that become challenges. Awareness can help you anticipate these challenges, but not always. Hindsight is 20/20, and compassion serves you well when you miss something that could have prevented a mishap.

- ♥ You want the best for your loved ones. Your relationships are the most important thing in your life. They give your life meaning, emotional support, and joy. Any opportunity to contribute to other people's lives is a gift that teaches you about yourself and ultimately improves the quality of your life.

- ♥ Awareness can lead to a "breakthrough" conversation and a new relationship with your family or loved one where you collaborate on care. Take advantage of this focus on loving, caring, and respecting all family members. You may ultimately be the primary caregiver for this person, part- or full-time, or you may become the "go-to person" for advice.

- ♥ The interest you show in your loved one's health and well-being will positively impact the family.

- ♥ Early identification of the problems can prevent delays in treatment or access to a clinical trial.

- You won't miss the opportunity to collaborate with your loved one to organize and plan for their future. As your loved one's health or memory and decision-making abilities decline, working together to organize and update medical, legal, and financial documents becomes increasingly difficult. A delay in this process can result in significant challenges for the family during a crisis. (See Part VI, Mistake # 16, 17)

- Uncertainty causes stress, and your anxiety will continue to increase until your observations are validated.

- By paying attention to warning signs and acting on observations, you avoid the guilt and regret of not acting sooner.

- **Why is paying attention to the warning signs important to you?**

Why Paying Attention To The Warning Signs May Be Difficult

- It can be uncomfortable to broach sensitive subjects. Be clear about your concerns so that you will communicate with intention, empathy, and respect. Think about your desired outcome and stay focused on collaboration. If possible, get confirmation from your loved one that *they* realize something is changing. Then, encourage them to engage with you honestly about creating an action plan.

- Your loved one may react unfavorably to having a conversation and may perceive your concern as an invasion of privacy. In addition, fear or embarrassment may drive resistance to further discussion.

- Your memory isn't always reliable, especially under duress, so continue to validate and document your observations. Approach conversations with respect, curiosity, and empathy so that you can respond rather than react when you meet resistance.

- You may question yourself. It's normal human behavior to deny or question what you have observed. Your mind might be saying, "Geez, something is not quite right here," but you put it on the "back burner" while at the same time, your heart is saying, "I don't want to upset the apple cart, but I love this person dearly," and you take action.

- You may recognize that you need to do something but don't know where to start. In that case, do not beat yourself up for indecision or not wanting to address the situation out loud. Be compassionate with yourself.

- It may be blatantly apparent something is wrong, but your loved one is not ready to admit it or discuss it.

- You may be in denial because you fear what the warning signs signify. Fear can be at the root of your resistance and inaction, as well as that of your loved one. It can be devastating to observe that your loved one's ability to function is changing. These observations can be painful and frightening when you don't have a plan or guidebook.

- You care about your loved one's well-being, and it may be difficult to stand by when you believe you know best, but it is important to allow your loved one to make their own decisions. You can offer support without forcing your opinion on them.

- **Why is paying attention to the warning signs difficult for you?**

ACTION PLAN:
Pay Attention To The Warning Signs

1. Set a baseline and document observations. When you are in a family member's home, observe their residence's condition. Is it untidy or unclean? Is that different from the usual? If living with the person, you will notice things that aren't quite right. For example: Mail—unopened and stacked? Bills—paid or piling up?

2. Date and document any atypical behaviors your loved one is demonstrating. You may not consider yourself a caregiver at this point, but ultimately, you could become one. This documentation will give you a timeline for events, health issues, and conversations.

3. Ask yourself, "Given the situation I've observed, what's the worst that could happen if I don't take action?" Write your answer in your journal or the *21 Mistakes Workbook*.

4. Then ask, "If I take action, what's the best possible outcome?" Write your answer in your journal or the *21 Mistakes Workbook*. Now, determine the actions available for each outcome and document this in your journal. The more you write down your thoughts, feelings, and action plans, the more you gain self-confidence, seek resources, and rely on your inner guidance.

5. If you have concerns, write them out. For example, is your loved one mentioning they lost their balance or had a fall? Who can validate the concerns? Avoid jumping to a hasty conclusion. Gain clarity on what you observed to confirm the reality of the situation.

6. Discuss your observations with a trusted family member to get corroboration or input.

7. Consider who else should be present when your concerns are validated, and you have decided to begin the conversation.

8. Outline the conversation, your objectives, talking points, and the response you expect to receive.

9. Choose a time to talk when you and your loved one are relaxed and at ease.

10. Sit with your loved one and let them know you want to help them prepare a medical emergency plan. Assure them that you are happy to show them what is involved and to assist them. This activity includes documenting medical history and medications, updating or creating legal documents, obtaining advice about finances and planning for medical costs. For creating a Care Community™ see Part IV, Mistake # 11.

11. Your loved one may already be aware of their situation but has postponed seeking medical attention. Remember that a decline in daily skills is the precursor to a loss of independence, and nobody wants that!

12. Use language that indicates your love and concern for the individual and that you want to be supportive. Be respectful of your loved one, their opinions and feelings concerning the matter, and their decision to act or not.

13. Ask your loved one open-ended, non-judgmental questions about what you've observed. You could start with a general inquiry, like, "How are you getting along these days?" and "I notice you're walking much slower than you used to. Let's discuss options if you need help around the house."

14. Avoid making assumptions. Even though the conversation may not result in any immediate action, you've started the talk and planted the seed. You cannot force people to do things

against their wishes just because you think you "know better." (See Part V, Mistake # 13)

15. What support can you, other family members, or friends offer? You might ask, "What is one thing I can do for you to be of assistance?"

16. Offer to be available when they need to talk. Check in on your loved one regularly by phone, video conferencing, or in-person visits to reassess the situation.

17. Be patient with people as they determine what is best for themselves. Put yourself in their shoes.

18. Their decision and behavior may impact your life in a stressful way. Find a way to arrive at a care situation that serves both of you.

Please visit www.HOCToni.com/actionplan/
for a free download of this Action Plan.

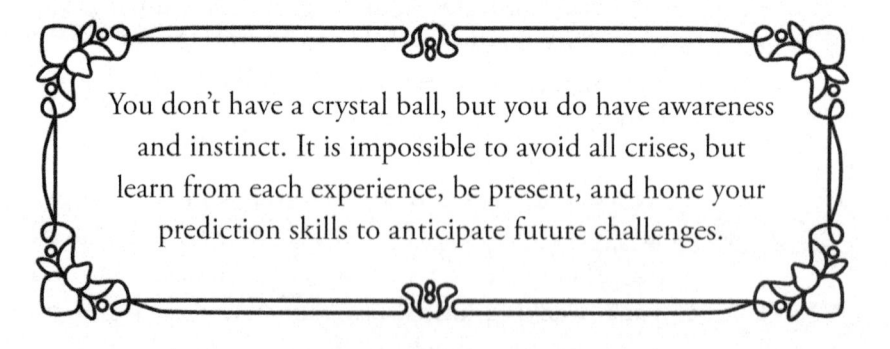

You don't have a crystal ball, but you do have awareness and instinct. It is impossible to avoid all crises, but learn from each experience, be present, and hone your prediction skills to anticipate future challenges.

Denial is comforting. It swaths you in layers of protection. When you are dealing with something so incredibly scary and difficult, it offers a buffer between you and the reality of the situation. Denial allows you to regroup in a way, but you can't stay there forever.
—Kimberly Chiozza Bridges
Diagnosed with Multiple Sclerosis at age 30

MISTAKE # 5

DENIAL: THIS CAN'T BE HAPPENING

Caregiving for someone with a life-threatening or progressive disease is a roller coaster ride of unending questions and emotions you don't want to or can't deal with now. When you receive an illness diagnosis for your loved one, it can seem unreal, and you struggle to believe it is really happening. The future is uncertain, you are in unfamiliar territory, and the fear can paralyze you, making planning almost impossible.

Once you have accepted your loved one's diagnosis, it is not uncommon to question if you are the best person to be the caregiver. You may even ask yourself over and over if you are doing it right. There's trial-and-error and failure, chaos, and it is exhausting. There is so much to learn, including many new medical terms. You often feel frustration and anger for being judged on how you are providing care for your family member. For many, there's sibling rivalry and disagreement on a parent's or loved one's care. You give so much of yourself, but it never feels like enough. Guilt and shame permeate your caregiving experience even though you have done nothing wrong to feel that way.

Caregiving can be one of the most challenging periods of your life, making it a tremendous opportunity for growth. When you accept your circumstances, that you are the right person for the caregiving role and recognize that each struggle is a chance to improve your situation, you turn the corner from victim to empowered caregiver. Otherwise, denial paralyzes you. Embracing challenges empowers you to overcome obstacles and gather the strength to continue your journey confidently.

When you embrace your role and situation, you open yourself up to experience the love, hope, joy, celebration, and memories alongside the pain.

Give yourself some grace as you and your loved one deal with a challenging situation. How you react to a serious or life-threatening diagnosis may depend on your thoughts and beliefs about our healthcare system, the degree to which you trust your doctor, and how it will affect all the plans you've made for your future. It's normal to be in denial. The diagnosis may unkindly and possibly dramatically interrupt plans. Take a deep breath and let the circumstances sink in. Information is power. Help your loved one seek out information that is helpful for an understanding of the health issue, treatments, options, outcomes, and next steps.

You may be so focused on managing the task and staying strong for your loved one that your emotions have not surfaced. However, note that eventually, you must deal with your emotions. Family members will each be managing their feelings in different ways, and the mix of uncertainty and fear can create a huge stumbling block when circumstances require the family to come together on decisions.

> I arrive for my routine annual mammogram, for which I have no concerns about the outcome. However, when the exam is over, the technician consults the specialist. She returns and tells me, "You need additional testing. Make a return appointment as soon as possible." I comply with their wishes and return within the week. I'm usually not concerned about test results, but my intuition cautions me that this is different. After the next test, an abnormality is confirmed. My primary physician refers me to an

oncologist who tells me the diagnosis is Left Breast Lobular Carcinoma Nottingham Grade 2, Stage 1. I am shocked that I have breast cancer, with no family history or prior symptoms. I now add "oncologist" to the list of my physicians and schedule surgery for the first available opening.

Yes, indeed, I am in shock. Yes, thrown off my game. Yes, scared by the diagnosis. At age 68, I live alone, and I consider myself a patient and my own caregiver. I am venturing into new territory, and I don't like it at all. I put my emotions on hold, figuring I will deal with them after the surgery! After all, worrying serves no purpose. As difficult as it is to dismiss, the outcome is uncertain, and maybe it will be fine.

Interestingly, months earlier, I booked a vacation to Alaska with the Dementia-friendly cruise where I am often a speaker. However, on this trip, I travel as a participant in the conference. It was good timing because when I tell my friends on the staff about my new diagnosis, they take good care of me.

When I return home and have the surgery, my friends are very helpful and share caregiving duties after the surgery until I can care for myself. I accept the diagnosis and follow up with my oncologist every six months.

This example of a diagnosis could stop anyone in their tracks. Any delay and the cancer could have progressed to Stage 2. While cancer is common, there are also rare diseases you have never heard of, and I have one of those too. It's called Myasthenia Gravis, which is hard to deny—the first symptom is double vision. It gets your attention immediately and doesn't go away on its own. Sometimes the symptoms are in remission; however, there is no cure. Should I worry about the progression? Not really; it serves no purpose. Should I plan for a possible progression and care that I might need? Yes, absolutely.

*Let's explore why moving from denial
to acceptance is important,
why it may be difficult, and how you
move from denial to acceptance.*

From Denial To Acceptance: Why It Is Important

- ♥ Acceptance gives you a sense of control and the ability to manage the moment and plan your lives while taking action in response to the diagnosis of a loved one.

- ♥ Acceptance provides the opportunity to have a vibrant life, live in the present, and tackle one challenge at a time. Life will be full of challenges, especially as you age and have unforeseen health issues. The disease doesn't define the person.

- ♥ Moving from denial to acceptance allows you to share authentically from your heart with family and friends. You create positive interactions and inspire support. With your most difficult challenges, you grow and find strength and gifts previously untapped.

- ♥ Inaction can delay treatment and prolong worry and stress. You avoid guilt and regret when you take timely, informed action.

- ♥ A life-changing diagnosis or event tosses your emotions into turmoil. Your feelings need to be acknowledged and addressed to avoid the consequences of worry and stress manifesting in your minds and bodies. The sooner you move to acceptance, the sooner you manage your emotions in a healthy manner.

- ♥ When the crisis hits, it's too late to plan for the crisis because it's already here. Decisions made under duress are often not the best decisions.

- ♥ **Why is moving from denial to acceptance important to you?**

From Denial To Acceptance: Why It May Be Difficult

- No one likes bad or scary news that can even derail a person with a mostly positive attitude. Depression, anxiety, worry, and stress are natural at the moment and afterward. You don't want to believe that the diagnosis or unfavorable situation is true, and you hope the outcome will change if you wait long enough. You spend time wondering and worrying rather than taking a big step into the unknown.

- Change is challenging and stressful. Stress from lack of knowledge about the disease or illness and its progression disrupts your daily routine, quality of life, and plans. If this disease progressive? How long will this person live? How long will you have to care for them?

- You don't know the next step or where it will take you, and it is less scary to stand still rather than take that step into the abyss.

- You are exhausted from worry and conflict. At some point, possibly after arguing for days or weeks or months, you and your loved one finally agree there may be a health issue, and you go together to the doctor to get an opinion. There may be referrals to specialists and tests such as an ultrasound, X-ray, MRI, and bloodwork. You are confused as you decipher pretest instructions, impatient and exhausted waiting to get tests scheduled, waiting and worrying about test results, and finally, waiting for the appointment where you get the diagnosis and treatment.

- The most feared outcome becomes a reality, and you are not ready to face it. Finally, you receive confirmation that there is something, and it's not normal—it's exceptionally lousy news. You and your loved one both have an emotional reaction. It's not what you hoped for, even slightly suspected, and NOT what you wanted to hear. Your initial response may be disappointment, shock, fear, or anger. These reactions and feelings are a normal response to an abnormal situation.

- Uncertainty or mistrust can inspire inaction. Your gut reaction is to dismiss the news because you are grasping onto your life as you currently know it and the life of your loved one. You may need help with what to do with this information. Do you recoil and give it time to sink in? Or do you grab the bull by the horns and act? You may ask, "Why is this happening? Why my loved one? Why now and what now?"

- You might stuff down all the feelings and decide not to deal with them. As a care professional once said, "Your heart will hurt!" You cannot "macho" your way through the caregiving experience, especially if it lasts for any length of time. It is a potential disaster in the form of poor health waiting to happen. When rundown by physical or emotional exhaustion, it may be difficult to help anyone, so you must address your pain and grief. In addition, your loved one has their own emotional experience.

- **Why is moving from denial to acceptance difficult for you?**

ACTION PLAN:
Accept Reality

1. Avoid being incapacitated by overwhelm. A good response is to take a deep breath and sort through the information your physician gave you and your loved one (hopefully, you took notes). In the USA, you can access test results and doctor's notes in your patient portal associated with the healthcare system. Review them as needed.

2. Openly discuss the diagnosis and how you feel about it with your loved one and family. Let them express their opinions and feelings about how to move forward. Help your loved one explore their thoughts and feelings to make necessary decisions.

3. What is the first action that you need to take? Is it to ask a question, do more research, or agree to a procedure?

4. Start two journals now. One to document medical decisions, treatments, and outcomes—one for you to record your experience, thoughts, and emotions. And continue to document your action plan in the *21 Mistakes Workbook*.

5. What research do you need to do right now? (Understanding the diagnosis, disease, progression, treatment, options, and clinical trials.)

6. Weigh the evidence supporting the diagnosis. Share the information with family and friends that you trust and ask for their opinion. They may offer objective evidence of behavior or condition in your loved one that they have observed that you haven't noticed. You may have a friend who has been through this illness or disease and can give you firsthand experience and offer helpful guidance.

7. Will a second opinion make you or your loved one more comfortable? If you or your loved one desire a second opinion, get it.

8. When ready, contact local and national organizations, such as disease-specific agencies, that can provide information. Record names and contact information for future reference. When ready, research and list online communities that can provide help and support.

9. With your support, input, and reassurance, your loved one can determine what treatment is best. However, if they are mentally incapable of deciding, it now falls to you or the individual designated as their Health Care Surrogate.

10. Ask for a commitment from a family member or friend to support you when you become emotionally stressed. It will be helpful to have identified a person to listen to you rant and rave, tell your story, and listen as you express yourself. Who will listen without judgment? Rarely is it a sibling, though it could be. It might be a family member or a person of faith. This person could be someone you hire who understands your experience as a caregiver: a Certified Caregiver Consultant™, therapist, or social worker. It should be someone you trust so you can be authentic about your feelings.

11. Decide on the responsibilities of your role as caregiver, and based on what you know about the illness or disease, begin creating a plan.

Please visit www.HOCToni.com/actionplan/
for a free download of this Action Plan.

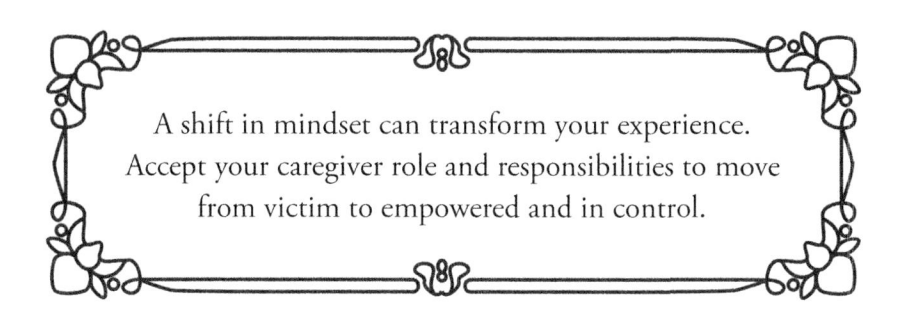

> A shift in mindset can transform your experience.
> Accept your caregiver role and responsibilities to move
> from victim to empowered and in control.

*You're knocked down, tired, disillusioned, disappointed.
Ask, what's one small step I can take to move forward?*
—Sasha Sabbath, Entrepreneur, Intuition and Purpose Soul Coach

MISTAKE # 6

DECIDING IT CAN WAIT

Caregiving requires making many decisions, some complex and some simple. We all process information at different speeds. Some may prefer to discuss the situation and possible solutions with a friend or professional to reach a decision, and some rely on intuition—all work, and I recommend all approaches.

In your caregiving role, you might face hiring help, finding a new doctor, adding a new medication, changing a dosage, or considering new living arrangements. Perhaps your loved one has just received a diagnosis of a serious illness, and the doctor has presented treatment options. When you receive a lot of information at once, the fear of making a mistake can be paralyzing. Urgency and heightened emotions (yours and your loved ones) contribute to feelings of being out of control. You can become overwhelmed by the choices and the gravity of the responsibility. Over time, frequent decision-making can result in decision fatigue.

The key to countering decision fatigue is to move forward one small step at a time. What is the next bite-sized piece of information you need to help you make the decision? Perhaps you weren't given the proper resources for support. Who can answer questions that will lead to solutions? What online resources can provide direction? Focus on the next step, and soon you will have reached the next decision-making level.

In January 2022, I have a severe cough for a week and test positive for COVID-19. My neurologist directs me to the hospital, where the X-ray shows severe pneumonia. I am on oxygen, and on the second day of hospitalization, one of the doctors asks if they should put me on a ventilator if the situation worsens. As she sits beside the bed having this conversation with me, I hesitate even though I thought it through before this hospitalization and prepared an answer. Since the doctor doesn't fully explain what is involved with being put on a ventilator, if necessary, I don't answer immediately. She says she will come back in 24 hours for my decision. When I entered the hospital, the possibility of death had not even entered my mind, but now it is real to the doctors, so I have to factor it into the equation. Wow, I didn't see that one coming! I really must be sick! No more thinking about an answer; circumstances require a decision.

A conversation later that evening with my partner helps clarify that we have questions and need more information.

The next day, when the doctor returns, I ask the questions and the answers lead me to say, "Yes, put me on a ventilator if it comes to that." Making a quick decision under stress adds to my anxiety. Unable to have my partner in the hospital to advocate for me because of COVID-19 restrictions, conversations with him on the phone comfort me and help me make the right decision. It turns out that the ventilator isn't necessary. I recover surprisingly quickly and return home with oxygen in two weeks. Sometimes you don't get to procrastinate on decision-making!

Let's explore why taking action is important, why it may be difficult, and how you move from inaction to action.

Why Taking Action Is Important

Gathering information from a variety of sources will guide you and your loved one toward the timely and appropriate decision that is best for them and you.

- ♥ Treatment options for a disease may become limited as time passes, or you may miss opportunities to slow the progression.

- ♥ Lack of or incomplete legal documents poses significant issues if your loved one becomes incapable of expressing their wishes or, worse yet, dies before they record their wishes. However, the Executor of the Will must carry out the recorded wishes, even if the loved one changed their mind yet didn't update their Will. (See Part VI, Mistake # 16)

- ♥ Caregivers can miss opportunities for assistance by postponing decisions. For example, your loved one's adjustment may become more difficult, moving from home to an assisted living or memory care facility.

- ♥ Following a period of inaction, you will experience relief from worries and stress with an increased energy level when you decide to take action.

- ♥ You will enjoy increased confidence in decision-making.

- ♥ **Why is taking action important to you?**

Why Taking Action May Be Difficult

With such a big learning curve and many difficult decisions, even small ones can feel insurmountable when you are new in your caregiving role. In addition, some circumstances and decisions are much more painful and challenging than others. For example, consider a spouse with early onset Alzheimer's Disease and their caregiver completely exhausted from years of care at home. How does one decide if it is time for a memory care facility? Your challenge is to assess every situation, evaluate all possible solutions for benefits and risks, get as much support as needed, and make the decision. Think of every decision as a small step forward.

- Decisions surrounding care often require conversation and collaboration. When a change is imminent, emotions heighten, and consensus can become more challenging.

- Financial options are narrow, and no one in the family can step up.

- Limited care options for home care and waiting lists for facilities.

- Any change in daily routine is upsetting for yourself and your loved one.

- Accepting that your loved one's independent days are over.

- Making such significant changes can prompt guilt over making wrong decisions.

- **Why is taking action difficult for you?**

ACTION PLAN:
Take Action

Many factors may cause inaction, and it is easier to overcome the obstacles and take action when you accept the situation by exploring and addressing uncomfortable feelings. Check in with your intuition or pray, and assess the options and the pros and cons. Gather your resources, talk to friends you trust, speak to professionals who can help, and do your research. Most importantly, consult with your loved one and help them create and implement a plan based on the current circumstances. Be sure to include them in the conversation with professionals, being mindful of not talking about them in the third person in their presence.

Multiple conversations will assist in making each decision. When you demonstrate care and compassion and maintain a spirit of collaboration and respect, it is easier to reach a consensus. The goal of each conversation is to keep lines of communication open. Determine what is preventing you and your loved one from deciding. Use the following steps as a guide when facing a difficult decision.

1. How are you feeling? Are you afraid, angry, upset, confused, or overwhelmed? It's normal to be constantly on edge about the uncertain future.

2. Maybe you're worried it's the wrong decision. Gather as much information as possible to feel comfortable understanding the current problem.

    a. Discuss the information with your primary care physician, specialist, or other health care provider, and obtain their recommendations.

    b. Get a second opinion if you need one. It could be from a doctor if it's a medical decision, a financial advisor or accountant to plan for future costs, or a friend who had to make similar decisions.

    c. Do your research on the internet from trusted websites, the library, and national organizations.

    d. A senior helpline in your community can provide resources for you.

e. Join a support group and get information on how others have managed this issue.

   f. Ask family members for their opinion. Then listen. Refrain from dismissing their view if it is different from yours. Avoid arguing or defending your position on the matter. Let them know you appreciate their input and will consider it.

3. Eliminate the options that offer the least benefit.

4. After limiting the number of options, consider each one individually. For each option, list all the positives, negatives, or risks. Make a thorough list and set a timeframe for deciding.

5. Follow your intuition, spiritual, or religious guidance.

6. Above all else, discuss options with your loved ones and find out their preferences. Then, if either of you still has questions, go back, and review the suggested solution.

Common Caregiving Scenarios That Involve A Difficult Decision

1. **Driving**

   Is your loved one driving safely or endangering their life and the lives of others? Has there been a recent accident or several that could have been preventable? Driving is the first step toward a lack of independence, which is challenging for you and your loved one. Before you decide for them, prepare for the future by asking your loved one, "What would you want me to do if I have a concern about you driving safely, but you don't agree with me?"

2.   **Downsizing**

Downsizing the home for a change in residence is another consideration. Typically, people want to stay in their homes because their home is a source of comfort, memories, safety, and certainty. However, staying in their home may no longer be a good option, primarily because it may have become an overwhelming burden on you, the caregiver. Before your time caring for the person increases beyond your capabilities or endurance, ask them, "If you should suffer an illness and I am concerned about you caring for yourself in your home, or I cannot realistically care for you in my home, what would you want me to do?"

The solution may involve moving in with your loved one, your loved one moving in with you or another family member, hiring an in-home caregiver, moving to a retirement, assisted living, or memory care facility, or asking other family members or friends to help.

3.   **Advanced directives**

In today's healthcare environment, the topic of advanced directives is a reasonable point of discussion. Ask your loved one, "If a severe case of COVID-19 or pneumonia or other condition puts you in the hospital, what are your wishes for life support?" Obtain the required documentation if they do not wish "heroic measures."

4.   **Clinical trials**

Clinical trials look at new ways to detect, prevent, and treat disease. Most people know very little about what might be involved. Ask your loved one, "If you develop a disease such as Alzheimer's or Parkinson's or something progressive, would you be interested in signing up for a clinical trial?" Assure them that you will gather more information before helping them decide.

Please visit www.HOCToni.com/actionplan/
for a free download of this Action Plan.

> Gather information, and consult with experts, family members, and your loved one for their input. Keep in touch with yourself, your inner guide, and your source of strength. Help your loved one make the decision. You will feel a great sense of relief and can begin to plan the next steps knowing that despite inaction, progress is possible.

PART III

YOU DON'T KNOW WHAT YOU DON'T KNOW

*In our culture, we have no relationship with not-knowing.
But not-knowing is the essence of receiving.*
—Mary Saunders, Founder of the low-cost
Community Acupuncture Clinic
Boulder, Colorado

Your mindset can radically affect the course of your life. Overwhelming research on mindset shows that the way you think about yourself and the world around you can drastically change the way you learn, how you handle stress, how you create success, your resiliency, and even how your immune system functions.
—Chopra.com

MISTAKE # 7

NOT SHIFTING YOUR MINDSET

Few of us have caregiving experience as we grow up, except to watch our parents care for their parents or have a sibling with special needs. Otherwise, you may have given caregiving little thought. You may only realize your preconceived ideas about caregiving are inaccurate once you are in a crisis and you are the one who needs to take charge. Then, forced to examine your *perception* of reality and preconceived ideas about caregiving, you can begin shifting your mindset and redefining what it means to be a caregiver.

When I accepted care responsibilities for Mom in 2003, I didn't know what I was getting into and how all-consuming it was to become. As the years of caring for her went on, my biggest challenge was overcoming the nagging belief that there was always one more thing I *should* be doing to make Mom comfortable, assess her medical condition, and bring her a better quality of life. I caused myself a lot of stress, and I eventually learned to say to myself, "I've done enough today. Mom is good. I am good." Shifting my mindset allowed me to relax and appreciate our time together.

My introduction to caregiving begins in 1989 unexpectedly. My parents are preparing for retirement and being away from the office in Florida, so they are at their condo in Las Vegas, Nevada. Over breakfast, Dad tells Mom, "The best is yet to come." Later that night, while enjoying the casino, there are no warning signs when my dad suddenly slumps over the poker table while Mom is at a slot machine. She hears a commotion, and that's how she finds out her husband has died. That night, I am in Houston on a business trip, and one of our employees calls me at 2 am in the hotel room (before cell phones) with the news that my dad has died. After catching an early flight to Las Vegas, I join Mom at their condo. We are in shock. I make arrangements to get Dad's body from the funeral parlor. The airline comps our return trip to Orlando.

Since I am working with both parents in our family business, I can be with Mom throughout this transition, help her with the legal and financial details that accompany the death of a spouse, and be there for her emotionally without significant adjustment to my daily schedule. It is a harsh introduction to caring for a grieving parent with no idea what is ahead.

I own my home three miles from Mom's home but move in with her for several months to ensure she eats adequately and gets the rest she needs. I drive her where she needs to go. During this transition year, she asks me to promise to be there for her if she ever becomes ill and needs my assistance in her "old age." I agree on the spot.

Fourteen years later, in 2003, I fulfill my promise. I move home to be with Mom. Caregiving starts simply enough with small chores and morphs into moving Mom to an assisted living facility (ALF) after a life-threatening illness. Even with the help of staff at the ALF, in my mind, I am still on call 24/7. I stay home for fear the ALF staff will call me and I will need to manage a health crisis. The calls are minimal compared to the number of hours I wait for the phone to ring. However, thinking I need to be on call day and night causes a massive disruption to my quality of life until I change my mindset and attitude.

Accepting my responsibilities includes being honest with Mom about my exhaustion and helping her understand my need to set boundaries. For example, instead of spending time with her every day at the assisted living facility, we talk on the phone some days. Instead of running three errands some days, I schedule one chore or doctor visit. Instead of postponing my doctor appointments, we discuss my health and include my priorities in our scheduling. She understands that supporting me helps me to support her! Mom also understands that I devote my Wednesday nights to my Toastmasters Club, as I need to be with friends and continue sharpening my speaking and leadership skills.

Through honest conversations, we shift our mindsets to embrace all we have to learn about this new experience. I feel calmer, Mom feels more included in my life, and we open ourselves to the joys of the opportunity for a meaningful caregiving journey together.

Here are examples of beliefs that can interfere with accepting the caregiving role:

- It's not my job. The oldest sibling or one who lives closest should care for Mom and Dad.

- I am an only child, so I *have* to be the caregiver.

- I don't have a good relationship with my parents, so this will never work out.

- I live in another state, so I can't care for anyone.
- I wasn't the favorite child, so that won't work out.
- I'll have to put my life on hold to care for this person.
- There's no way they will do what I tell them to do. They are too stubborn.

Here are examples of beliefs that can interfere with feeling empowered in a caregiving role:

- There is no time for taking care of my well-being.
- I don't have time to see a doctor for a minor ailment or schedule my regular wellness appointment.
- I guess feeling exhausted is normal.
- I must take care of my loved one before I take care of myself.
- I must get through today.

A substantial percentage of caregivers die before their care recipient! Here are examples of beliefs that will help you thrive in your caregiving role:

- If I take care of myself first, I can better care for my loved one.
- A consistent morning routine is an excellent way to start my day, for example, stretching for 2-3 minutes, mindfulness exercise for 2-3 minutes, having a healthy breakfast, and reading religious or inspirational material.
- Asking regularly what type of help my loved one needs.

- I don't have to do everything myself. Who else is available to assist?

- What are the resources for hiring help?

- What help do I need to make time for caregiving, for myself, and other commitments?

- I approach caregiving with a positive mindset. I welcome the opportunity to help a loved one.

- Caring for this person may be a gift I don't yet recognize.

*Let's explore why shifting your mindset is important,
why it may be difficult,
and how you can shift your mindset to regain control.*

Why Shifting Your Mindset Is Important

- ♥ When you are curious, ask questions, avoid being reactive, and accurately assess your situation, you experience improved health and happiness.

- ♥ Where do you start when caregiving is uncharted territory and you don't have a map? If you begin with false preconceived ideas about your path forward, you will be lost before you start your journey. Awareness of your misconceptions is a step in the right direction and becomes a part of your growth process.

- ♥ Holding on to preconceived beliefs can cause resentment resulting in added stress. Shifting your mindset reduces stress and opens you to the possibility that you have a lot to learn. With this knowledge, you make intentional decisions that serve your loved one and all who will be involved in caring for your loved one.

- ♥ When you seek new perspectives and opportunities that may require reaching outside your comfort zone, you discover more about yourself.

- ♥ Shifting your mindset can positively impact your relationships with family members or siblings. As a result, you expand your ability to give and receive love.

- ♥ **Why is shifting your mindset important to you?**

Why Shifting Your Mindset May Be Difficult

- Caring for a loved one does not have a definitive timeline, and an open-ended expedition can be daunting, causing you to resist a shift in your perspective when you don't know the length of your commitment.

- You may not have chosen this role, yet you feel obligated to take charge due to someone's health crisis.

- You may believe caregiving is about telling your loved one what to do rather than collaborating to help them remain as independent as possible for as long as possible. Your misdirected approach will prevent you from providing the needed support, and you will feel like you failed when they reject your assistance.

- You often make assumptions about what others expect from you, causing you to miss out on the joy of relationships and, thus, the rewards of life.

- **Why is shifting your mindset difficult for you?**

ACTION PLAN: Shift Your Mindset

1. Is immediate help needed? How will you address your loved one's current needs?

2. Identify and explore your beliefs about caring for your loved one, including any thoughts causing you to resist accepting care

responsibilities. Hidden beliefs may be the root of resistance, so you may need help to resolve them.

3. Explore the benefits you will receive when you shift to a more positive view of your caregiving experience.

4. Have conversations with your loved one about their needs and what role you might play. Ask questions and indicate your love and support. These discussions will help everyone avoid assumptions.

5. Caregiving requires a time commitment. Determine if you have adequate time to devote to care responsibilities. If your obligations to others or job responsibilities already consume much of your time, consider who would be better as the primary caregiver. Be aware that once you become a caregiver and as priorities shift, finding balance in your life becomes more challenging.

6. While one person typically invests the most time in caregiving tasks, part-time caregiving assistance is a big help, even if you live in another city or state. Will your contribution be a support role? Identify ways you can help the person who is the primary caregiver.

7. As caregiving needs intensify, assess the situation and consider who can join your care team to help you care for your loved one. Family members? Friends? Neighbors? Begin conversations with these folks to determine how each person can contribute.

8. Please give family members, friends, and neighbors a copy of this book.

9. Locate the information and resources that can help you manage caregiving responsibilities that speaks to your current situation and throughout caregiving. Be open to asking for help and expanding your support network.

10. Seeking help or guidance from someone who has been a caregiver will give you the confidence to make crucial decisions.

11. Learn and practice effective communication strategies for positive interactions. (See Part V, Mistake # 13, 14)

12. Take the time to understand caregiver responsibilities. (See Part III, Mistake # 8)

Please visit www.HOCToni.com/actionplan/
for a free download of this Action Plan.

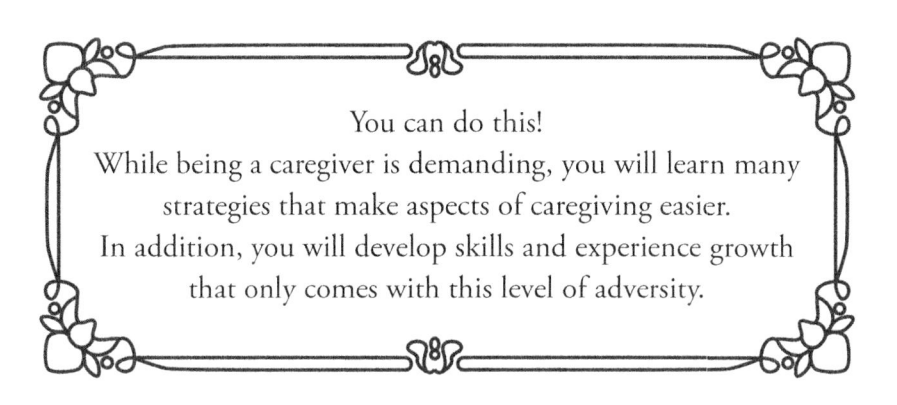

You can do this!
While being a caregiver is demanding, you will learn many strategies that make aspects of caregiving easier.
In addition, you will develop skills and experience growth that only comes with this level of adversity.

Doctors diagnose, nurses heal, and caregivers make sense of it all.
—Brett H. Lewis, author of *Family Caregiving*

MISTAKE # 8

NOT KNOWING YOUR NEW RESPONSIBILITIES

At some time in your life, you probably have had the experience of being a short-term caregiver, even though you didn't use the term "caregiver." For example, you may have taken care of a family member or friend in the comfort of their home while they recovered from a hospitalization or surgery. Maybe you helped someone who was recovering from the flu. While these care responsibilities take your attention away from your usual activities to some extent, they do not require the time, energy, and accompanying stress needed to take care of an individual with a chronic illness or progressive disease.

Circumstances around the caregiving experience vary from person to person, and long-term care can significantly interrupt your life. You may wish your new responsibilities came with a guidebook to help you identify the ever-evolving, seemingly endless tasks.

I once gave a speech in my Toastmasters Club about caring for my mom. Even though caregiving is a serious topic to most, it was supposed to be a humorous speech. At that point, I had been caring for Mom for several years and was able to find the humor in my caregiving journey.

It started something like this:

"You know what a caregiver is, right? Have you heard of 'Driving Miss Daisy'? Mom's name is May, and I'm driving Miss Maisy. And she is driving me crazy! I am an errand boy, entertainment director, and project manager. I schedule and take her to doctor's appointments.

I oversee her financial, legal, and business dealings. I am her Health Care Advocate and medication manager. I do her laundry, give her showers, feed her, and take care of her dog. Or maybe I take feed the dog and take care of her. I guess I do both! I lose track after a while!"

Let's explore why identifying caregiving responsibilities are important, why it may be difficult, and the steps you can take to identify them.

Why Identifying Your Caregiving Responsibilities Is Important

- ♥ Accepting care responsibilities for a loved one will provide the opportunity to have an invaluable life experience. You will rise to the challenge, grow personally, and appreciate the positive impact and joy of caring for another human being.

- ♥ Knowing and understanding responsibilities minimizes uncertainty and reduces feelings of being out of control. When you feel out of control, you experience frustration, anxiety, anger, and a lack of confidence.

- ♥ Preparation and planning can prevent some, though not all, crises.

- ♥ Failure to understand and manage care responsibilities effectively often results in neglecting your health and well-being, leading to long-term health issues. Thirty percent of caregivers die before the death of their loved one.

- ♥ Your Action Plan will save time and money and reduce stress and overwhelm.

- ♥ Increased knowledge is the beginning of power. Knowledge applied is your superpower.

- ♥ Develop good organizational skills.

- ♥ **Why is identifying caregiving responsibilities important to you?**

Why Identifying Your Caregiving Responsibilities May Be Difficult

- Integrating caregiving into your day can present a challenge. Your life is already busy with built-in stressors such as relationships, work, raising children, family responsibilities, and increasing cost of living. In addition, there are troubling world events, the COVID-19 pandemic, and divisiveness in the country, which all can consume you physically, emotionally, mentally, and spiritually.

- You may be unaware of how to accomplish all that is required and don't have enough information to make thoughtful decisions. Seek the information and resources you need to address your circumstances and help you make decisions.

- Learning on the job involves mistakes. Continue reading relevant "mistakes" in this book and create your Action Plan for each.

- **Why is identifying caregiving responsibilities difficult for you?**

ACTION PLAN:
Know Your Responsibilities

As you become a full-time caregiver, you may have many of the following responsibilities. Check responsibilities you are currently doing.

CHECKLIST OF RESPONSIBILITIES

Medical

- ✓ Keep a medication and health history spreadsheet or list, update it as needed, and share it with all health care professionals.

- ✓ Refill medications.

- ✓ Pick up medications at the pharmacy or arrange for delivery.

- ✓ Sort medications.

- ✓ Remind your family member to take medications.

- ✓ Schedule doctor appointments.

- ✓ Take your family member to the doctor and provide for other transportation needs.

- ✓ Observe your family member between appointments and make a note of health issues or concerns to discuss the next time you accompany them to the doctor.

- ✓ Develop a list of questions to ask the doctor.

- ✓ Review with your loved one what the doctor said.

- ✓ Research a disease or health issue.

- ✓ Discuss recommendations for care, tests, or treatment.

- ✓ Help a loved one make medical decisions.

- ✓ Make medical decisions because your loved one is unable to.

- ✓ Prepare a medical emergency plan.

- ✓ Depending on the health issue, the nursing staff may train you to do several procedures at home for your family member (for example, they taught me to do wound care).

- ✓ Evaluate the need for a Call Alert bracelet or necklace.

Non-Medical

- ✓ Help with dressing.

- ✓ Help with bathing.

- ✓ Help with toileting.

- ✓ Assistance with mobility. Transferring wheelchair to toilet.

- ✓ Research the local, state, and national resources, the local Area Office on Aging, a Certified Caregiving Consultant™, Senior Advisor, or Case Manager.

- ✓ Interview and hire home companion help.

Household

- ✓ Run errands.

- ✓ Grocery shopping.
- ✓ Other shopping.
- ✓ Plan, cook, and clean up after meals.
- ✓ Take your loved one out to eat.
- ✓ Laundry, ironing, taking clothes to cleaners.
- ✓ House cleaning.
- ✓ Fix things around the house that break.
- ✓ Maintain the yard.
- ✓ Take care of a pet.

Financial

- ✓ Make sure that bills are paid or pay the bills.
- ✓ Keep and organize important records and documents.
- ✓ Make financial decisions.

Family

- ♥ Communicate with family members, hold family meetings, and delegate responsibilities because you are the communicator-in-chief.
- ♥ Provide emotional support.
- ♥ Companionship.

- ♥ Daily or regular visits if living separately.

- ♥ Take care of your well-being and family or children while taking care of your family member who needs care. (See Part IV, Mistake # 10, 11, 12)

Social

- ✓ Entertain and provide activities.

- ✓ Organize visits from friends.

- ✓ Organize and coordinate birthday parties, holiday planning, and special events.

✓ BREATHE

Consider using this checklist of responsibilities to create your action plan (and ask for help):

1. Determine how you will organize caregiving responsibilities. Do you prefer a checklist? Spreadsheet? App? Website?

2. Identify the tasks your loved one can do.

3. Identify the tasks you do.

4. Identify the tasks you think others might do.

5. Identify the tasks to hire out.

6. Talk with family and friends and let them select tasks they are comfortable completing.

7. Revisit the checklist of responsibilities and update your caregiving plan frequently by setting a reminder when there is a change in abilities, hospitalization, or decline in cognitive capacity.

8. Compile a list with contact information of people your loved one knows and people you know who are currently assisting you or who you can ask for assistance.

Please visit www.HOCToni.com/actionplan/ for a free download of this Action Plan.

> When you start a new job, you receive a job description. When you become a caregiver, you must create your own, updating it as circumstances evolve. You are your boss, so set yourself up for success and make a comprehensive list.

*If there's one thing I've learned in life,
it's the power of using your own voice.*
—Michelle Obama, Former First Lady of the United States

MISTAKE # 9

NOT SPEAKING UP TO AUTHORITY

When interacting with health care professionals, your loved one may or may not be able to speak up for themselves. Because you are attuned to your loved one's needs and listen from a different perspective, you can be an enormous support. You'll notice if the physicians and health care professionals address their needs fully. Your support is significant during a doctor's appointment, emergency department visit, hospitalization, or any interaction with a health care professional.

People we look up to and trust, like physicians, often have limited time to spend with their patients, especially in a hospital setting where they hurriedly make rounds. In addition, while they are focused on caring for the patient, they are not necessarily communicating with the patient or the family member caring for the patient.

Do not get discouraged if doctors and health care staff don't include you in a conversation about a family member you've brought in for care. However, it is an opportunity and *the time to speak up*. Unfortunately, some professionals do not realize that the caregiver is an essential care team member and that their insights and observations are valuable for care.

If you feel that the health care provider is ignoring your input, use your voice to establish your role as the expert in your family member and a valuable part of the care team. Demonstrate respect as you advocate for your family member.

Advocacy involves knowing your loved one's wishes and asking for what is best for them during each interaction, asking for clarification when something isn't clear. Advocacy is also asking for water, ordering meals, a bedside commode, a discontinued medication to be resumed because you know it will be beneficial, asking the doctor what time they make rounds in the morning so you can be there, asking the reasons for the treatment they are giving, and requesting the prognosis.

Insist on being involved in decisions as the care partner of your loved one. You are an "essential" caregiver!

> Mom is in the hospital on numerous occasions. I always focus on three areas: 1) making sure to the best of my ability that Mom is receiving good care, 2) talking to her doctors to get information and ask questions, and 3) advocating for Mom and even offering suggestions to the doctors, reminding them of medications that did or didn't produce the desired results in the past.
>
> I spend hours in the hospital waiting for doctors because Mom cannot communicate with them as thoroughly as I can or, on occasion, at all. Some doctors make their rounds in the hospital at regular hours, but it can vary from day to day. Thus, at times, I spend the entire day in the hospital, requiring me to find care for my dog because I refuse to leave the hospital for fear of missing the attending physician with the latest update. Some may say it isn't necessary; however, with so many mishaps that can and do happen in hospitals, I feel more comfortable, and Mom feels safer with me there.

A loved one's hospitalization can be exhausting for the caregiver, so it can be helpful to have a trusted friend or family member as an alternate advocate. Then you get a break, rest, or attend to other responsibilities.

Let's explore why becoming an advocate is important, why advocating may be difficult, and how you can advocate for your loved one.

Why Becoming An Advocate Is Important

- ♥ Accepting your position as an advocate is fulfilling your responsibilities as the primary caregiver and care team leader.

- ♥ Being prepared, demonstrating knowledge, and establishing rapport with health care providers positions you to be the voice for your family member when they can't advocate for themselves.

- ♥ Even when your loved one can advocate for themselves, hospital settings and stressful doctor's appointments are ripe for mistakes and misunderstandings. A second set of ears and eyes will help ensure the most successful outcomes.

- ♥ Communication and advocacy are keys to getting your loved one what they need in a timely manner.

- ♥ Finding your voice as an advocate builds your confidence and solidifies your place at the head of your loved one's care.

- ♥ When others hear what you have to say and value your input, your frustration and anger dissipate.

- ♥ If incapacitated, your loved one relies on you to understand the doctor's instructions and the care plan and make decisions.

- ♥ When you model advocacy behavior, you help the next caregiver be noticed and included in the conversations with health care professionals.

- **Why is becoming an advocate for your loved one important to you?**

Why Becoming An Advocate May Be Difficult

- The very people you need to interact with ignore you, and you can feel intimidated speaking up to these trained professionals.

- Your frustration and anger may have set the tone for the interaction, and they may dismiss you because of your behavior.

- You might be concerned that you are unqualified to advocate for your loved one or worry that you will make a mistake or miss something.

- **Why is becoming an advocate for your loved one difficult for you?**

ACTION PLAN: Advocate For Your Loved One

1. What steps do you need to take to prepare for interaction with any health care providers involved in your loved one's care?

2. Get in touch with your insecurities. How do you feel about your role as an advocate for your loved one?

    a. On a scale of 1-5 (1=low, 5=high), what is your ability level to advocate?
    b. What help or assistance do you need to get to level 5 advocacy?

3. Organize medical information. The more knowledgeable you are about your loved one's health history, medications, past illnesses, surgeries, vaccinations, and physician contact information, the more likely you are to engage medical professionals in effective conversations, so they take you seriously.
(See Part V, Mistake #15)

4. Get even more organized. Carry a notebook of medical information about your loved one. Include legal documents and let the physicians know you have Health Care Power of Attorney or Health Care Surrogate if your loved one should be unable to communicate their wishes. Have reports of significant tests and diagnoses at hand. Be prepared to recap the purpose of the visit or what led to an emergency room or hospital admission. Electronic documents are helpful. However, having a paper copy is easier for the professional so they can immediately read the info that validates the reason for your visit or relevant history. Keep results of tests and any pertinent documentation as part of a care plan.

5. Tell health care professionals that you are responsible for carrying out their instructions and scheduling any follow-up visits for care. You can tell them you are a family member and emphasize you are the patient's essential caregiver.

6. With respect, speak up assertively and listen attentively to engage in productive conversations. Your advocacy is essential to the well-being of your loved one. Developing and maintaining relationships is critical to being a strong advocate. Speaking up can feel uncomfortable. The more you practice, the easier it will get. Remember, it is a huge responsibility to care for another human being. You are now a "caregiver advocate-in-training," and your responsibility includes your loved one.

7. Express gratitude and share that you consider the professionals important on your loved one's care team and appreciate their cooperation with you.

8. NEVER leave an interaction without all your questions answered. Remember always to use a calm voice. If you are unsure what to say, try this: "I know you would feel better knowing I have all my questions answered before you leave."

9. Who can you ask for help or to accompany you and your loved one to the next doctor's appointment or emergency department when a crisis occurs?

Please visit www.HOCToni.com/actionplan/
for a free download of this Action Plan.

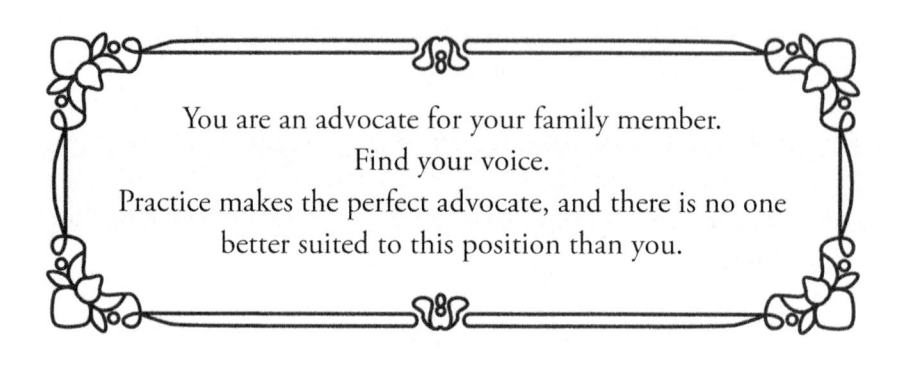

You are an advocate for your family member.
Find your voice.
Practice makes the perfect advocate, and there is no one better suited to this position than you.

PART IV

YOU DON'T PRIORITIZE YOUR WELL-BEING

Basic principles from a Jewish Perspective:

1. *You need a support system. It's not good for a human being to be alone. You need to be connected to people.*

2. *You need to open yourselves up to love and opportunities for healing.*

3. *You need to be present to all of your emotions. Work with it, cherish it, embrace it, have compassion for it and you will grow.*

4. *Because actions of positivity have a very powerful impact on our heart, our soul, our psyche (love, kindness, generosity, giving, benevolence), get accustomed to engaging in rituals that are loving and kind.*

—Rabbi Yosef Yitzchak Jacobson,
Chabad Rabbi and Teacher

Self-care is a multi-dimensional way to consciously engage in activities that promote healthy functioning. It's about taking time away from your normal daily commitments and activities to take care of yourself… Self-care is about checking in with yourself to see what you need for an optimal state of being. It's about nurturing the opportunities to slow down, be present, and have gratitude for the life you are living.
—Diana Raab, Ph.D. *Psychology Today* online edition July 8, 2022

MISTAKE # 10

FAILURE TO PUT YOUR OXYGEN MASK ON FIRST

When you care for a loved one, their needs can be so great that you understandably prioritize their well-being to your detriment. Unfortunately, when you neglect self-care, you may become exhausted and burned out. There is a lot of "doing" in caregiving. Sometimes you forget to breathe. You may think, as I did, that your first responsibility is to your loved one. However, it must be to yourself, so you provide the best possible care without endangering your health and life. Consider these five categories of self-care as we explore why self-care is essential.

Physical – Nourish your body with healthy eating, hydration, movement, and rest.

Emotional – Process your emotions. Journaling, counseling, and expressing creativity can positively impact your emotional well-being. Improve your social well-being by nurturing healthy, positive connections and a sense of belonging by fostering dynamic friendships, love, support, and intimacy.

Mental – A flow of ideas and learning can inspire, challenge, illuminate your mind, and teach you about yourself and your world while showing you what is possible.

Spiritual – Nurture yourself spiritually by spending in nature, cultivating a positive mindset, and living purposefully. Even when silence, solitude, and simplicity are unavailable, you can connect with a higher power, wherever you are and whatever you're doing, through mindfulness. Religious or spiritual practices can enhance your well-being. Consider prayer or meditation on a regular basis.

Practical – Establish routines for you and your loved one. Use a to-do list and your calendar or another method for increased productivity. Practical activities include meeting with a financial advisor, creating a budget or a plan to pay for care, scheduling, making and attending appointments, running errands, and managing transportation.

> After several years of caregiving Mom, I am painfully aware of every minute, every hour, day, week, and month that goes by that all I seem to do is take care of her. If I am not directly caring for her, I am thinking about caring for her or worrying about her. All my attention and energy are on giving to Mom. I feel like I have lost my sense of self. I feel as if my world is closing in on me.
>
> At the same time, I can't imagine not making it my #1 priority to take care of Mom. Well-meaning friends repeatedly tell me that if I don't take care of myself first, I will not be able to care for Mom effectively. Unfortunately, I plummet so far down the rabbit hole that I don't have the energy and can't imagine how to do it. I know I am not eating well and that I have gained weight. I have been a caregiver for so long, devoted to Mom, that I accept how I feel as the new normal and don't realize the impact it is having on my health and my life and how the

stress is robbing me of my happiness. Meanwhile, I feel criticized, judged, and frustrated that my friends can't understand my struggle.

The first challenge is convincing myself that prioritizing my well-being is paramount. Sadly, I almost hit rock bottom before making a change. The second challenge is figuring out what self-care looks like for me and how to fit it into my busy schedule with Mom, which swamps me.

Part of the stress of being a caregiver is you feel the weight of the responsibility of caring for someone who cannot fully care for themselves. In addition, you may insist on doing things for your loved one rather than figure out what they can do for themselves, which would require patience. However, if you can let go of control, they will enjoy a sense of accomplishment and the dignity of independence, and you will get a break. Letting your loved one take responsibility for their care needs can also reduce conflict. Nevertheless, continually assessing their ability is stressful.

Hopefully, you have a friend, close confidant, or caregiver consultant who will be honest in assessing your situation to help you focus on caring for yourself without sacrificing the level of care you provide for your loved one.

Let's explore why prioritizing your well-being is important, why it may be difficult, and what steps you can take to make it happen.

Why Prioritizing Your Well-Being Is Important

- ♥ Self-care can be life-changing and a key to your survival and happiness.

- According to the Caregiver Action Network, as many as 70 percent of caregivers exhibit clinical depression, with many taking prescription medication for anxiety. In addition, family caregivers experiencing extreme stress age prematurely. This stress level can take up to **ten years off a family caregiver's natural life**.

- Failure to put yourself first can cause serious health issues for YOU! Many caregivers report being sleep-deprived, exhausted, never getting a break, and expressing concerns about depression.

- When you neglect and bury your emotions, including disappointment, upset, anger, self-doubt, self-hatred, overwhelm, anxiousness, guilt, fear, depression, and resentment, these emotions take a toll on your physical and emotional well-being.

- Neglecting your well-being leads to isolation, inability to make decisions, procrastination, low energy, low sex drive, exhaustion, and a loss of joy and passion for living.

- Increases the ability to think and communicate effectively and make difficult decisions.

- Prioritizes your well-being and creates a sense of calm, peace, serenity, confidence, enthusiasm, energy, joy, and happiness.

- Being present in the moment and make and treasure the memories of this time with your loved one and the caregiving journey.

- Finding purpose and meaning in your caregiving journey.

- Reaching out to share your journey with friends who may find value in your experience.

- **Why is prioritizing your well-being important to you?**

Why Prioritizing Your Well-Being May Be Difficult

- Are you working and raising a family? Are you a solo parent? Or are you an only child with a full-time career when your parent suddenly needs help? When a situation calls on you to be a caregiver, you already feel like there are too few hours in the day.

- You have no idea how long your role as a caregiver will go on, which is daunting.

- You have pre-formed ideas about self-care and think such activities are spa treatments and luxurious weekends away. You don't recognize that self-care is any activity that helps you feel whole and can be as simple as taking a coffee or tea break.

- Self-care can feel like another "to do" when you are overwhelmed.

- **Why is prioritizing your well-being difficult for you?**

ACTION PLAN: Prioritize Your Well-Being

(See Appendix 9 for a list of activities by self-care category.)

1. Set an intention to prioritize your well-being and create and implement a self-care plan so that you prioritize self-care *before* it feels like an impossible task.

2. Review the self-care activities list and consider each with a fresh perspective, exploring each practice with an open mind.

Which activities could renew your energy or relax your mind and body? Highlight the ones you want to explore more.

3. Reflect and consider your needs in each of the five self-care areas.

    a. List one suggestion in each area that will make the most difference in your life.

        i. Physical
        ii. Emotional
        iii. Mental
        iv. Spiritual
        v. Practical

    b. Identify and schedule one small action you can take in each area that will improve some aspect of yourself, your mood, or your outlook on life.

        i. Physical
        ii. Emotional
        iii. Mental
        iv. Spiritual
        v. Practical

4. Create a plan that allows you to take small steps. Some ideas:

    a. Each morning, set a daily self-care intention.

    b. Take a mini-break every hour.

    c. Set the alarm to help remind you.

    d. Each evening, assess your progress.

5. Write down your progress in a journal or in the *21 Mistakes Workbook*. What activities worked to help you feel better? What

practices didn't have an impact on your well-being? Adjust your plan accordingly. It takes time for each new step to impact your well-being, and these observations can help you track progress and motivate you to continue to experiment and discover your self-care formula.

6. Identify an accountability partner in each of the five self-care areas. It's more fun with a partner and enhances your emotional well-being. Who can help you commit to and continue your self-care efforts?

7. If you are hesitant, do the required research to locate any resources that will help you take action and move forward.

Please visit www.HOCToni.com/actionplan/
for a free download of this Action Plan.

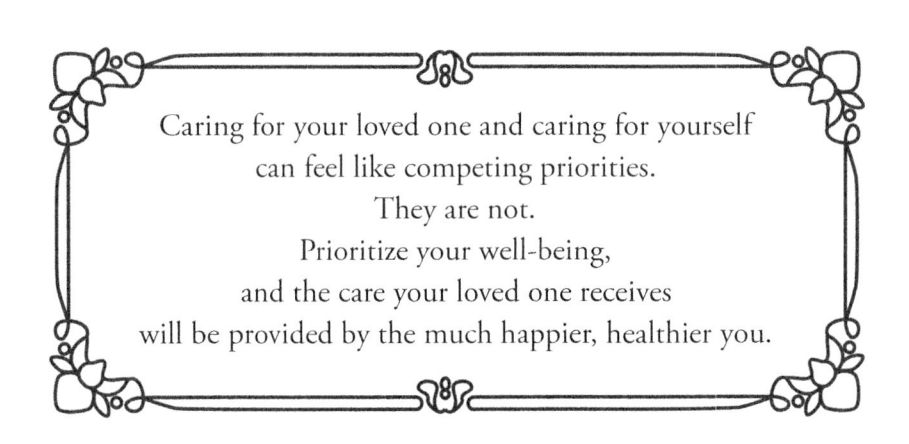

> Caring for your loved one and caring for yourself
> can feel like competing priorities.
> They are not.
> Prioritize your well-being,
> and the care your loved one receives
> will be provided by the much happier, healthier you.

*I knew I had a problem. I thought I could
solve everything myself. I can do this.
I'm intelligent. I'm wealthy I'm rich. I'm successful, why can't I do this?
I come and for 16 years I couldn't say, "I need help," you know that?
Those three words that will save your life. I need help.
If you're in pain and you're afraid to reach out
but because you think people think you are weak,
if you feel ashamed of asking for help, just swallow your pride.
Your pride will kill you.
Just ask for help and people will be there to give it to you.*
—Elton John, Entertainer, YouTube interview with Oprah Winfrey:
"The Three Words that Could Save Your Life"

MISTAKE # 11

YOU DON'T ASK FOR HELP

Now that you've learned so much about your loved one's health and lifestyle, you are probably correct in thinking that you are the best one to care for your loved one. However, that doesn't mean you are the *only* one. You may not realize there are consequences if you try to do everything yourself. Typically, caregiving doesn't get easier; it gets more complex. It doesn't take less of your time; it takes more time. You don't get less stressed; you get more stressed.

> As an only child, the entire responsibility for caring for my mom falls to me, and I gladly accept it. Caring for Mom involves making decisions, establishing routines, entertaining, scheduling appointments, talking to doctors and health care professionals—in other words, everything.

After trying to care for Mom in her home for several months, I realize that if I care for her alone, I will give up my life entirely to manage care responsibilities. I can't imagine how one person can do it all.

The decision early on to place Mom in an assisted living facility (ALF) is the best decision. It supports me to still be a "daughter" to Mom. I never feel guilty as it seems we both get the support we need, and a better quality of life for us both.

However, the worst decision is acting like I still have to be a 24/7 caregiver. I think I am taking care of myself by hiring extra help to be companion care for Mom. However, I still feel stressed because when I am not with Mom at the ALF, I sit on my couch at home, exhausted most of the time, waiting for the phone to ring with the next emergency.

Driven by the fear of regret of overlooking what I can do, I do everything possible to keep Mom happy and healthy. I am proud of how I take care of her, but despite all the support of the assisted living facility, I wear myself out. Comfortable living alone and not in a relationship, I overlook my friends as a resource. As a result, my life becomes narrower, I schedule less and less time with friends, and I give up meaningful pursuits and regular activities that used to enrich my life.

With Mom in residence at the ALF for eleven years, my "professional help" expanded to include the staff: nurses, certified nurse assistants (CNA), the activities director and her team, physical and occupational therapists, and physicians who serviced the facility. In addition, I considered the dining room employees part of our community. Mealtime was also a social activity; the staff loved getting to know the residents and finding out how they were doing. With many friends, Mom's social life blossomed. Later, the hospice staff became a part of our care team, including nurses, social workers, CNAs, rabbi, and a chaplain.

> By year eight, however, I am losing it big time. As much as I want to spend quality time with Mom, especially when she is healthiest and at her best, I begin to feel I *should* always be "on call" for her. I feel guilty when I want to do something else, and she wants time with me. Mostly, though, I give in to her wishes, not knowing how to deal with the guilt, or put my needs first. I need relief.
>
> While the certainty of death and uncertainty of timing intensifies with age, right from when I recognize Mom's increasing health issues, I struggle to set boundaries for myself about her eventual death. How will it happen? Will it be today? I think I should go to see her in case this day is her last. Seemingly a loving gesture, I am naively motivated by having no regrets, which is understandable, except I overlook regretting how poorly I care for myself.

Meanwhile, Mom was hospitalized with a life-threatening condition and willed herself *back from death* three times!

> She seems so strong. Sometimes I wonder if she will outlive me, especially with my stress level and poor self-care habits. Eventually, I realize I need to set boundaries, and the surprise is that Mom is instantly agreeable to what I need. She sees the toll caring for her is taking on me.

Only some have the financial capability or insurance to provide paid care. You may not know to plan for care, and as you get older, your options become more limited. I suggest creating a Care Community™ for you and your loved one so that you are not alone with care responsibilities.

Let's explore why asking for help is important, why it may be difficult, and when to ask for help, and build your Care Community™.

Why Asking For Help Is Important

- If you don't get the help you need, caregiving can devastate your health. Your self-care may deteriorate. You gain or lose weight, stop exercising, or have some illnesses, and you worry about how you can go on and survive this experience. Statistics support that **30% or more of caregivers die** before their loved one.

- When you try to do it all yourself, anger and resentment build. You can resent the person you're caring for and others you think should offer help or who do offer support and then don't meet their commitment.

- You feel isolated, which may result in despair, negativity, depression, poor health, and the inability to make effective decisions. Stress robs you of the joy you might otherwise create in your caregiving experience and relationship.

- Caregiving can be exhausting, when you are responsible for so many aspects of your loved one's care. You are their emotional support and may even have saved their life a few times. It is not uncommon to question, "when will this end?" and then feel guilty for having that thought.

- Keep in mind there are people eager to help and will appreciate giving their support, as it brings them joy, satisfaction, and purpose. Remember to ask!

- Caregiving becomes a shared and more fulfilling experience with others who also create memories with you and your loved one.

- ♥ Accepting help expands your interaction with people and deepens relationships with new and current friends and family members. These interactions may develop into life-long, caring, and intimate relationships.

- ♥ Expanding your loved one's interaction with supportive people and, thus, their social network brings greater happiness and less dependence on you.

- ♥ When you accept help, you have more time to focus on yourself, your needs, and your health. Your big pay-off is your well-being and sanity.

- ♥ Setting guidelines and boundaries regarding your time and activities with your loved one can reduce resentment and increase your happiness and joy as a caregiver.

- ♥ **Why is asking for help important to you?**

Why Asking For Help May Be Difficult

- While you may believe you are the best person to care for your loved one, you are not the only one.

- Accepting help requires reframing your belief that it means additional work when someone else is involved.

- You worry about what people will think about you if you ask for help.

- You have asked for help, and people have disappointed you.

- Someone helping in your loved one's care may do a better job than you are with more patience and a better response, so jealousy arises.

- **Why is asking for help difficult for you?**

ACTION PLAN:
Ask For Help, And Build Your Care Community™

---

1. Reflect on why asking for and receiving help may be difficult and why you hesitate. Explore your beliefs about what you were told or taught about asking for help. Why have you decided you are the only one who can and knows how to care for your loved one? (See Appendix 9)

2. See Appendix 5 to build your Care Community™ of potential and current helpers representing your caregiving plan and lifeline, including their specific tasks and responsibilities. It will serve you well, especially if your caregiving lasts years instead of weeks or months. Recognize that sometimes the same person can assist in multiple capacities!

3. Create your Care Community™ and invite people to join with a specific role. Let the people on your list know how much you appreciate them and the value of their help and support. Create this document at the beginning of your caregiving journey so that negativity, overwhelm, and lack of energy don't become your default way of dealing with caregiving.

4. Identify the tasks you are willing and able to delegate or share. In Mistake # 8, you made a "Checklist of Activities" with the tasks your loved one can do for themselves, tasks you do for your loved one, and tasks others can do for both of you. You can use that list to get started. Sometimes, you may need to accept that someone does not do their task precisely as you would. Be open to the possibility that they might do it even

better. Either way, remember that you benefit from more time for yourself, so don't stress about someone doing better than you. Enjoy it!

5. Identify one person who you trust and who you can talk to regularly and give them a call. If that person is agreeable, set up a schedule to talk, meet in person, or chat online as needed. It may help if that person is a current or former caregiver, although, most importantly, they are willing to support you.

6. What emotional support would be helpful from a professional? Locate a therapist, counselor, religious or spiritual leader, or caregiving consultant who can help you explore ways to lighten the emotional and physical caregiving load. There is a community of Certified Caregiving Consultants™ trained to guide you through your caregiving experience. Most, including myself, offer a complimentary consultation to answer your questions and get you started in the right direction. Meanwhile, keep reading this book as a do-it-yourself project.

7. Locate community resources that you can employ to reduce your caregiving or personal workload.

8. Find and take time to participate in an online or in-person support group. It's not selfish; having a place where you can speak freely and confidentially in a community of like-minded people is essential. It might be a social media community, a chat room, a community website, or an in-person meeting.

9. The person you care for needs social interaction. Identify people who will visit and set up a schedule (and ask them to bring food or a treat). Remember to address expectations around time for both sides. For example, don't balk at people willing to spend only 30 minutes because that might be perfect for your loved one and still a break for you. On the other hand, someone

hesitant to visit may enjoy it more than they anticipated and stay longer. Be grateful for their willingness to show up.

10. Who can join you in your quest to care for your loved one? Begin to list every person involved in some aspect of care, including those who currently support you and those who could help you. Include their name, contact information, and the assistance each can provide you or your loved one.

11. The list you develop is not a one-and-done exercise. Continue to add and subtract people as you engage health care providers, family, friends, neighbors, and others you will meet. As your loved one's medical needs increase, you will meet new doctors, for example. Or a friend will surprise you and one day ask if there is anything they can do for you. Always answer, "Yes!" and add them to the team. As you start asking for help, it will get easier. Your community will expand.

12. If you can engage your loved one's help, all the better, as you become Care Partners.

Please visit www.HOCToni.com/actionplan/
for a free download of this Action Plan.

Go for the triple win or the triple G!
Letting others help is a Gift to them, a Gift to you,
and a Gift of someone new for your loved one.
Accept help, lead your care team, and use the time and
energy you gain to focus on your well-being.

Do something. If it works, do more of it. If it doesn't, do something else.
—Franklin D. Roosevelt, past President of the United States

MISTAKE # 12

YOU MISS OUT ON RESOURCES – DIDN'T GOOGLE IT

Caregiving support resources exist in your community, region, and state. There are also national resources. Today we are so fortunate with abundant educational materials, videos, books, websites, chat rooms, support groups, conferences, and businesses in the senior care and caregiving industry. Understandably, while your loved one's care needs are evolving, you do not yet know all the resources you will need. However, consider what could support your loved one and make your life easier and your health better before a health crisis—not the ideal time to begin. So begin now when things are calmer.

Acknowledging up front that there are things you don't know about how to be a caregiver will empower you. You are often on your own to navigate the healthcare system and locate resources, so it is helpful to learn to ask good questions.

I assumed my background as an instructor at Baylor College of Medicine and my ability to establish good working relationships with doctors was all I needed to know. While it was a HUGE plus having had experience working with and educating doctors, I needed to learn how to ask the right questions about treatment options for new-to-me health issues to help Mom make effective decisions.

Some of the specialists we needed were neurology, orthopedics, wound care, urology, infectious disease, oncology, and pain management. Since I was "old school," I relied on conversations with doctors and health professionals for information who didn't often provide local resources. However, Mom received more care and support once in the assisted living facility.

When your loved one is deteriorating with a health issue, you focus on their treatment or services. Therefore, my mistake was not thinking about what I needed as a caregiver, so I was missing out on resources that would support me. I can't believe I didn't "google" more often to find information and resources that would help me.

Remember, you are part of a vast national caregiving community. Be curious and ask questions. Research. Connect with other caregivers. Participate in that community and reap the benefits of lessons learned from other caregivers. Find resources in your community, at the state level, nationally, and online that can support and help you in your caregiver role. Look for educational programs, respite opportunities, and services that can be beneficial in reducing stress and addressing your unmet needs.

Let's explore why locating resources is important, why it may be difficult, and how to begin finding them.

Why Locating Resources Is Important

- ♥ Having the necessary information is the antidote to worry, empowering you and helping you confidently proceed.

- ♥ Knowledge and information help you manage and prioritize your caregiving responsibilities.

- ♥ Someone who has walked in your shoes can guide you in moving forward and give you confidence in decision-making.

- ♥ With some effort, you can often locate one well-informed contact who can refer you to valuable services.

- ♥ Caregiver support groups are a great way to learn about available resources. When you attend a support group session, you are connected to the resources shared by fellow family caregivers and to the emotional support provided when you talk with people who understand what you are going through and can offer advice based on their caregiving experience.

- ♥ Locating resources before you need them prevents doing research during an unexpected crisis. Any disruption of your routine creates high stress, confusion, and uncertainty, which is not the best time to find helpful resources.

- ♥ If you don't do the research, you can miss out on the opportunity to build your support team, access clinical trials that might ultimately affect treatment, and share information and solutions with others going through a similar journey as you and your loved one.

- ♥ **Why is locating resources important to you?**

Why Locating Resources May Be Difficult

- Finding the resources that will be the most helpful can be challenging and time-consuming.

- Discerning conflicting information for reliable resources on your loved one's health issues may be difficult.

- Locating a support group that is a good fit may be challenging.

- Navigating the internet for information that you need can be frustrating.

- Information overload is real, leaving you confused and overwhelmed and needing a break to regroup.

- **Why is locating resources difficult for you?**

ACTION PLAN:
Locate Resources

---

1. What information do you need right now? Where can you begin to locate that information? Consider community resources and those online. What are the treatment options, and do you have enough information to develop a care plan?

2. Reach out to health care professionals with questions. Many physicians are now part of a health care group that may have an extensive website and resource section. Start there or ask your primary care physician and specialist about resources for your loved one and yourself. "What resources can you provide?" or "Can you refer me to someone who can assist with _____?" When should you schedule the next appointment?

3. Call your local Area Office on Aging for local resources. (https://eldercare.acl.gov/)

4. Consult with a Senior Care Manager or Certified Caregiving Consultant™.

5. Talk with friends who have been through similar challenges.

6. Identify and record local resources, national organizations, current health care providers, and caregiving and medical information websites. Even if you do not need help now, you might in the future, and keeping organized files can save you time and further research.

7. Join a support group and learn to network with fellow caregivers. When does your local or virtual support group meet, and who is the contact person? Write down the meeting information (day, time, location).

8. Learn to ask questions that elicit the information you need from people. If you are unsatisfied with an answer, ask for clarification, or rephrase your question. Persistence pays!

9. Google it! Get on your computer and do internet searches, check national organizations (related to a specific disease), books, and YouTube videos. Suggested searches: How to be a caregiver to a spouse. How to be a caregiver to my parents. Where is my local Area on Aging? What are treatment options for Ocular Myasthenia Gravis? What is MRSA? What is Stage 3 Breast Cancer? Where can I find a support group for cancer survivors? Support for caregivers? What questions should I always ask my doctor? How do I select an assisted living facility? Who are the home companion companies in my area? Just about any well-phrased question will lead you to resources.

10. Research can lead you to treatment options, clinical trials, or alternative care that may significantly affect your loved one's health and well-being.

11. For additional support in locating resources, enlist a Certified Caregiving Consultant™ at: https://www.thecareyearstrainingacademy.com/meet/

12. Review the Resource Section and then Google your questions for the necessary information.

Please visit www.HOCToni.com/actionplan/
for a free download of this Action Plan.

> It's never too soon to identify resources for your loved one and yourself to share with fellow family caregivers because you never know when you will need them.

PART V

INEFFECTIVE COMMUNICATION SKILLS

Most of the time, success in the world depends on collaborating with other people. And learning how to do that, learning how to listen, learning how to treat people with respect and with dignity, learning how to be humble ... those are the human qualities we all need in our everyday life.
—Doris Kearns Goodwin
American biographer, historian, political commentator

How a person seems to show up for us is intimately connected to how we choose to show up for them.
—Marianne Williamson, Author, *Return to Love*
spiritual leader and political activist

MISTAKE # 13

NOT KNOWING WHAT YOUR LOVED ONE NEEDS

You may believe you have become an expert in all health-related issues your loved one faces. You may think your opinion is correct without listening to their wishes, which is a typical first reaction. In assessing a situation, problem, or decision that requires action or a solution, you may jump ahead and make assumptions without first asking essential questions and listening to the wants, needs, and opinions of your loved one. Put yourself in their shoes for a moment and listen to what you are telling them to do. How would you react? Your eagerness to help can leave that person feeling unseen, unheard, and unappreciated. As a result, they may become angry, defensive, and argumentative.

When caring for an adult who can express themselves clearly, it is vital to have effective and meaningful conversations while they can still share their desires and wishes. The goal of these conversations is to build trust with your loved one, offer support and assistance, and build a loving care-partnering relationship.

> I am truly fortunate that Mom and I have a wonderful relationship. Caregiving poses many challenges for us, initially around her desire to remain as independent as possible and my desire to help her all the time. One day, after a brief argument around

my insistence that I get her a cup of coffee rather than getting it herself, I take a moment to reflect on the situation and put myself in Mom's shoes.

I can see her health deteriorating and know she is losing her independence. Meanwhile, despite my concern that she might spill the coffee while walking back to her chair, I recognize the importance of encouraging her confidence in doing this easy task. Mom gets her coffee, and she is happy. We have very few arguments after that.

Even though the coffee issue is minor, if unaddressed, such things can add to resentment and become an obstacle to solving more significant problems.

Asking about Mom's feelings and desires rather than imposing my wishes is essential to deepening our relationship, effective communication, and her happiness. Further, I consciously avoid judging her decisions, complaining about the circumstances, and using words that make her feel small and helpless.

When I am patient with Mom, communication is easy. I recognize that she looks to me to understand information about her health and relies on me to help her make decisions. For example, we look at options for treatment and make a list of pros and cons or benefits and risks. Then, we discuss the list until we agree on the plan of action that feels right. When unsure what to do, she appreciates that I take responsibility for initiating conversations to facilitate a solution and get things done.

Concerning legal documents, I spend hours ensuring she is happy with her Will's contents and her charitable donations.

When we plan our time together, I often give her a list of activities for her to choose, depending on her energy and mood that day. This collaboration works because she trusts me and relies on my support.

Let's explore why learning about your loved one's wishes is important, why it may be difficult, how to have productive conversations, and what you need to do to get started.

Why Learning About Your Loved One's Wishes Is Important

♥ When you learn about your loved one's wishes, opinions, and feelings, they feel seen and heard. With this knowledge, you can help them achieve their dreams and accomplish their goals.

- ♥ Listening attentively to each other lets you learn new things about what your loved one wants and believes. You may hear new ideas that you hadn't considered before.

- ♥ Avoid the frustration of repeating the same conversation without a resolution or an action plan by asking clarifying questions to understand why something is important to your loved one.

- ♥ You nurture and deepen love and respect when you listen to and validate your loved one's desire. Cultivate your communication strategies to engage with your loved one in a way that supports both of you.

- ♥ Knowing your loved one's wishes is crucial, so you don't make decisions based on assumptions that conflict with their desires.

- ♥ **Why is learning about your loved one's wishes important to you?**

Why Learning About Your Loved One's Wishes May Be Difficult

- Being disagreeable, argumentative, or opinionated about care can prevent learning important details about your loved one's wishes regarding where they live, how they live, and health-related decisions.

- You may have yet to learn to communicate with your loved one in a way that helps you both get what you need for now, tomorrow, and the future.

- You may not recognize the right and ability of your loved one to make their own decisions and therefore don't take the time to consult with them.

- You may feel resentful and unappreciated for all that you do for them. Your resentment could make you feel entitled to make decisions without learning and considering your family member's opinions.

- You may be exhausted and overwhelmed. Caring for someone and facing constant decisions and uncertainty creates all the feelings that drain your energy, such as guilt, frustration, hopelessness, helplessness, anxiety, worry, stress, and anger. You can be constantly upset, so it is out of the realm of your ability to take the time to have meaningful, thoughtful, and exploratory conversations.

- **Why is learning about your loved one's wishes difficult for you?**

General Conversation Guidelines

- ✓ Think of the relationship as a partnership and get curious about what your loved one wants and needs.

- ✓ To encourage your loved one to value your help, stay calm, don't take anything personally, be patient, ask specific questions to start the conversation, or further your understanding of their wants and needs.

- ✓ Make every effort to avoid interrupting your loved one while they are still expressing their opinion. Interrupting and making assumptions about what your loved one wants and needs can create conflict.

- ✓ Maintain sincere communication by asking open-ended questions. ("What do you need?" "What are your concerns?" "How does that make you feel?") Listen attentively and be respectful. If they are a person of few words, accept that they have said all there is to say for now. Or, give them choices, for example, "Are you happy or sad?"

- ✓ Give them your complete attention, and do not multitask!

- ✓ Speak from your heart and be honest.

- ✓ Allow silence. People need time to answer a question or formulate what and how they want to say something.

- ✓ Avoid blame, criticism, judging the person about what they are up to, or getting defensive and arguing for your position.

- ✓ Avoid raising your voice, making demands, or insisting they do things your way.

- ✓ Avoid falling into victim mode about past situations where you feel wronged and getting your feathers ruffled over differing viewpoints. Fully hear out your loved one and wait until they finish speaking.

- ✓ If you think they have finished talking or stating their opinion, ask, "Is there anything else you'd like to add?" Repeat until they say there is nothing else.

- ✓ Now it's your turn to give your opinion or feelings about the issue and respond to what they have said. Offer reasons for your view and point out their positive ideas. Focus on your points of agreement.

- ✓ Express kindness and gratitude. Say, "Thank you for having this conversation with me. It was beneficial."

ACTION PLAN:
Have Effective Conversations With Your Loved One

1. Review the conversation guidelines when planning and before each conversation until they become standard practice.

2. Reflect on the conversation you plan to have and describe it in your journal or the *21 Mistakes Workbook* and include why this conversation is important and what you hope to accomplish. Script the conversation or the points you want to cover.

3. Plan how you will manage the conversation to be non-argumentative, which includes taking responsibility for bringing up the topics, keeping your cool during the discussion, and guiding your loved one to the decision they prefer.

4. Let your loved one know you'd like to get their input and schedule a time to talk.

5. Share the conversation guidelines with your loved one if appropriate.

6. If you have done research or have notes from their doctor, have those available for the conversation.

7. Introduce the topic and purpose of the conversation and make any remarks for context. You could indicate that you understand it may be a sensitive topic, so it will be helpful to talk about it.

8. Discuss any ground rules that will be helpful such as not interrupting each other.

9. Start with an open-ended question that lets them state their opinion.

10. Take notes during the conversation, so you don't have to remember everything your loved one says.

11. If your loved one can decide about their care and insist on a particular path (and you believe they are not endangering themselves), consider that they have the right to choose their course of action, even if you disagree.

12. The first conversation about a situation may be just the starting point. Don't pressure for a decision or resolution of an issue unless timing is crucial. Be open to revisiting the conversation and agreeing to collect more information for a follow-up. Set a time.

Please visit www.HOCToni.com/actionplan/
for a free download of this Action Plan.

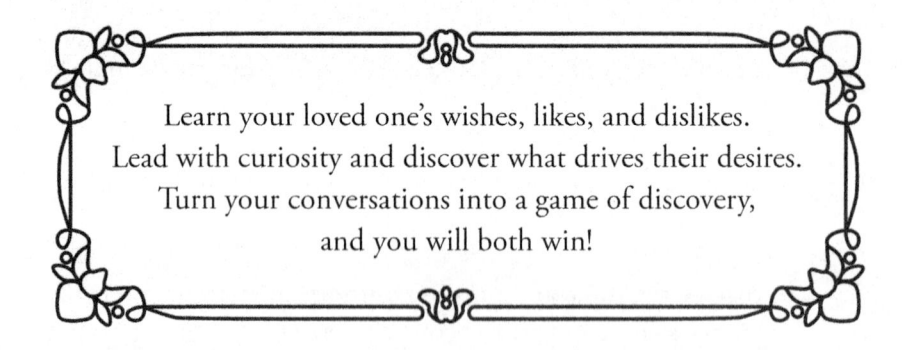

Learn your loved one's wishes, likes, and dislikes.
Lead with curiosity and discover what drives their desires.
Turn your conversations into a game of discovery,
and you will both win!

Caring for a loved one, no matter the reason, be it dementia or another health concern, can be all consuming and impact relationships deeply. Family dynamics often evolve. Sometimes people find a strength they never knew they had. In the best-case scenarios, it can bring families together, challenges are shared, forgiveness is given as need be, and gratitude is freely expressed.
—Mary Sue Wilkinson, Educator, professional musician, author, speaker, trainer

MISTAKE # 14

NOT FINDING OUT HOW OTHERS CAN HELP

Involving family and friends who support you and your loved one in the caregiving journey, while ideal, is not always possible. Don't feel discouraged; start talking with family and friends most likely to be part of your Care Community™. It is up to you to take the lead in asking for help.

Conversations create positive, caring relationships essential to increased happiness in your life. With a genuine desire to nurture and invest in the relationship, be open to learning more about friends and family. Share more about yourself and what you and your loved one need.

I often hear caregivers talk about feeling distant from family members who don't help, which creates rivalry and strife. They feel frustrated and angry by the criticism when they would prefer support. There may be resistance to having meaningful conversations or finding solutions to a problem, with any discussions feeling repetitive and draining.

One of the benefits of having Mom in an assisted living facility is the abundance of activities, special events around all the holidays, and parties. For example, Mom has many visitors, including a friend who has never experienced a Jewish holiday celebration. She wants to participate with us and my neighbors, who help us celebrate New Year's Eve. Friends and family come to Mother's Day brunch, and a friend joins us to enjoy the spirit of Cinco de Mayo. A former neighbor calls to schedule a lunch date, and we go out for pizza, or if Mom doesn't have the energy to go out, she orders and brings the pizza in. Long distance, Mom is supported by her younger sister, who calls on the phone almost daily. In addition, I have friends who meet me regularly for lunch or dinner.

Let's explore why it is important to include friends and family who can help and add joy and life to your days, why this may be challenging, and how to find the folks who will add value to your experience.

Why Asking For Help Is Important

- ♥ All the literature in positive psychology (the Science of Happiness) indicates that the happiest people in the world have caring and supportive relationships.

- ♥ Your relationships provide an opportunity to learn about yourself, your values, your strengths, your goodness, and your challenges for growth.

- ♥ When you nurture relationships, you build lasting, quality friendships and enjoy experiences that become the fabric of your most treasured memories.

- ♥ Your ability to reach out to others and welcome their relationships positively impacts their life.

- ♥ When you don't include friends and family in care, you don't offer them the opportunity to be involved.

- ♥ Your caregiving journey presents an opportunity to build a relationship that will continue. Otherwise, a missed opportunity can result in regret, guilt, sadness, or upset for not being able to foster a positive connection.

- ♥ Surrounding yourself with love and support helps prevent the common experience of loneliness and isolation often felt by a caregiver.

- ♥ You expand your Care Community™. (See Appendix 5)

- ♥ **Why is including friends and family important to you?**

Why Asking For Help May Be Difficult

- The need to overlook past hurts.

- Fearing that reaching out involves a lot of effort.

- Believing that some relationships are beyond repair.

- Not realizing the benefit of asking for and receiving help.

- Letting go of the belief that asking for help is a weakness.

- Fear that the conversation will involve criticism and judgment.

- **Why is including friends and family difficult for you?**

ACTION PLAN:
Ask For Help

---

1. List who you want to call.

2. Identify the objective of the call to each person and any challenges you anticipate. To minimize discomfort, imagine the conversation. For example, are you calling to ask their opinion, discuss a problem, or update them on the status of care? Prepare an open-ended question to begin rather than a question that involves a yes or no answer.

3. Contact the person, share the reason for your call, and offer any remarks you would like to make to set the stage for the discussion. Some suggestions on how to get started:

    a. I want your opinion about something.

    b. I want to discuss ideas with you.

    c. I'd like your help making a decision.

4. It's always beneficial for all parties to express their opinion, preferably in a calm, loving manner. Let the person know you want to hear from them and intend to listen without interrupting. Avoid assuming you know what they are going

to say. If you think they have finished talking or stating their opinion, ask what else they want to share. Then, listen to the end of their remarks.

5. When they finish speaking, it's your turn to ask more open-ended questions to get the detail and clarification you need to understand their needs, concerns, and feelings. Again, assumptions prevent you from truly listening and understanding.

6. Now, give your point of view and respond to what they have said. Once you start talking, welcome their interruptions, even if they disagree. That is okay because they feel more comfortable communicating after you let them speak freely. Let the conversation flow.

7. Stay calm and avoid being defensive over differing viewpoints or arguing for your position. Avoid blame, judgment, or criticism.

8. See their point of view and thank them for their positive ideas. Chances are you will agree with some of what they say.

9. This initial discussion may be the starting point for a series of conversations. Don't pressure for a decision or resolution of an issue unless timing is critical. Be open to revisiting the conversation or collecting more information for a follow-up discussion. You may want to list the additional information you need or want to discuss next time. If needed, schedule a time to revisit the conversation.

10. Be kind and express gratitude. "Thank you for having this conversation with me. It was truly helpful."

Calling A Person To Re-Connect And Establish A Better Foundation For The Relationship

1. People have many reasons for avoiding challenging conversations. For example, if you had a falling out, begin with the attitude that whatever happened, you each did the best you could with knowledge at the time. This approach avoids placing blame or feeling victimized.

2. Speak from your heart and with intention. If it's been a while since you've had a pleasant or meaningful conversation, or any conversation at all, you might say, "I apologize that I haven't had time to talk to you. I want to catch up if this is a good time."

3. Be curious. Listen and ask questions.

4. People like to talk about themselves, so encourage them to share. Some useful phrases: "That's so interesting. Tell me more about that" or "I'd really like to hear more about that."

5. Keep the conversation positive. "It sounds like things are going well, and I'm happy for you."

6. Look for areas of agreement.

7. Validate what they say to the best of your ability: "Given the circumstances, it's understandable that you feel that way."

8. Offer support, "I'd love to help if I can. What is one thing I could do for you today?"

9. You might recognize that some of what *you* are saying is what you wish they would say. That's okay because you are modeling a caring and supportive conversation. Your attention is on them, listening and helping.

10. If they ask about you and the person you are caring for, by all means, provide a factual update without asking for help, just a truthful assessment of what is going on in your life. Be sure to talk about something that is going well in addition to sharing the challenges. If they offer help or an opinion about anything you said, be curious and ask more questions to ensure you understand their viewpoint. Avoid saying things like, "No, that won't work!" or "You don't understand." Instead, suggest talking further at another time.

11. At the end of the conversation, thank them for their time and suggest you connect more frequently. Then, decide a mutually convenient time.

Please visit www.HOCToni.com/actionplan/
for a free download of this Action Plan.

> Gather Care Community™ members and start with your family. Match family members' skills and abilities with care needs or support. If a match isn't possible, move on. Resentment only holds you back, and remember; you are moving forward!

Doctors diagnose, nurses heal, and caregivers make sense of it all.
—Brett H. Lewis, Author, *Family Caregiving*

MISTAKE # 15

SETTLING FOR "DOCTOR-SPEAK" YOU DON'T UNDERSTAND

It's up to you and your loved one to obtain the information needed for the best health care. Your loved one may have countless doctor visits, hospitalizations, and several physicians—a general practice doctor, neurologist, podiatrist, oncologist, orthopedist, urologist, and more. Each specialist has unique terminology that can be complicated and confusing, making it difficult to understand.

How do you interact with health care professionals? Do you ask questions when something is unclear? Do you accept what they tell you even if you don't understand the treatment, possible side effects, reasons for the treatment, and expected outcomes? Unfortunately, physicians are often in a hurry and unaware that you need clarification. While it may be initially awkward, with practice, you will learn to ask the right questions until you understand the answers—it is essential.

I felt the most confidence in my caregiving skills when talking with Mom's doctors. I established my relationship with them through small talk and mentioned that I had been an instructor at Baylor College of Medicine. While helpful in gaining rapport, they often interpreted my position to mean they could use medical jargon during our conversations. I had to ask for clarification, advising them that my specialty was audiology, a non-medical vocation. Sometimes, doctors had a terrible bedside manner, especially in the hospital. They would speak quickly and then turn around to leave the room before I could ask a question. Once, I grabbed a doctor by his arm because he started to exit without letting me ask my questions. I had waited hours to talk to him and would not miss this opportunity. He gave me a very unpleasant look, so I apologized, asked my question, and got my answer. I recommend a less aggressive approach, when possible, but do what you need to do when advocating for your loved one.

Let's explore why asking for clarification is important, why it may be difficult, and how you can confidently speak with health care professionals to receive the information you need.

Why Asking For Clarification Is Important

- ♥ Less anxiety, being well-informed about your loved one's health issues and less worry about missing or unclear information.

- ♥ Accurately sharing information with other health care professionals on your loved one's care team.

- ♥ When accompanying your loved one to appointments, you can take notes, translate doctor-speak for your loved one, and facilitate their decision-making.

- ♥ Accurately report information to family members and friends.

- ♥ More positive outcomes in understanding the health issue for proper action and managing your loved one's health.

- ♥ **Why is asking for clarification important to you?**

Why Asking For Clarification May Be Difficult

- You may feel unprepared to interact with the doctor.

- If the doctor is pressed for time, they may not answer your questions.

- You are unsure what questions to ask.

- You may be intimidated by the doctor's demeanor.

- The information and responsibilities may overwhelm you.

- You may feel embarrassed not understanding their explanation.

- With many professionals involved, you may be unclear about who can best answer questions.

- **Why is asking for clarification difficult for you?**

ACTION PLAN:
Ask For Clarification

Ensure your loved one's notebook of medical history is current, including their medication list.

1. Prepare for your loved one's doctor appointments. List information you must tell the doctor and brainstorm with your loved one any questions to ask.

2. What questions do you need to ask the doctor now?

   a. Often a doctor offers several treatment options. If you ask, "Which one do you recommend?" you may not get a direct answer. Another way to ask a question is, "What percentage of the time do your patients choose option one? Option two?" or "What treatment have you found the most effective?"

   b. Having been to countless doctor appointments over fourteen years with Mom, I developed three favorite questions to ask the doctor:

      i. "What haven't I asked you, or what haven't you told me that I should know?"

      ii. "What haven't you told me that others ask you?"

      iii. "If this were your mother, what would you do next?"

3. Ask if you can record the conversation and also take notes.

4. Ask questions as soon as you need clarification. Ask the doctor to spell the unfamiliar words. It might be the name of the disease, a medication, or a treatment option.

5. Repeat what you heard, including recommendations or details about the care plan, to ensure your notes are accurate.

6. Questions you can ask:

   a. What do you think is causing the symptoms?

   b. Is there a treatment? What are the side effects?

   c. What does that mean?

d. Can you repeat that, please?

e. I'm unfamiliar with that word. How do you spell it, and what does it mean?

f. Can you explain that in layperson's terms?

g. Tell me again, what are the options?

h. When do you need an answer?

i. When do you want to see us again?

7. Do you know how to access the doctor's and hospital's website and patient portal where you and your loved one can communicate information and ask questions anytime and usually get a response within 24-48 hours?

8. See Appendix 7 on how to prepare for a doctor's appointment.

Please visit www.HOCToni.com/actionplan/
for a free download of this Action Plan.

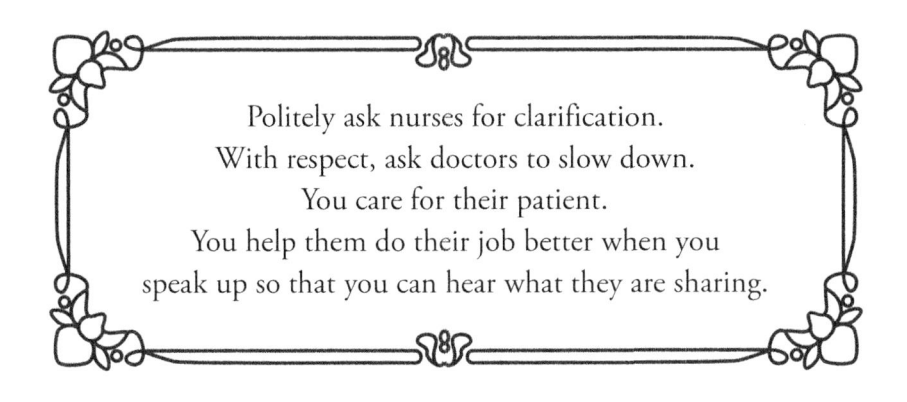

Politely ask nurses for clarification.
With respect, ask doctors to slow down.
You care for their patient.
You help them do their job better when you
speak up so that you can hear what they are sharing.

PART VI

NOT PLANNING FOR AN UNCERTAIN FUTURE

By failing to prepare, you are preparing to fail.
—Benjamin Franklin

*Know what legal authority you have.
Caregivers often have to assist a loved one with decision-making,
sometimes informally and sometimes formally.
Legal authority comes in three ways: through
powers of attorney for financial
And/or health care decisions; by default, through
surrogate laws for health decisions in many but not all
states; or through guardianship or conservatorship
proceedings in local courts, which should be a last resort.
Each of these pathways has different rules for the exercise of authority.*
—American Bar Association, Commission on Law and Aging

MISTAKE # 16

NOT HAVING LEGAL MATTERS IN ORDER

People are quickly and unexpectedly thrust into a caregiving situation without notice when a crisis happens. For you to step in and manage things for your loved one on their behalf, they must have prepared their final arrangements and assigned you as Durable Power of Attorney for personal care and property (designations differ by country, state, and province). If your loved one has designated you to perform this duty, but you have yet to discuss their wishes and don't know their preferences, you will be guessing rather than making informed decisions on their behalf. They should assign Durable Power of Attorney and personal representatives with care and consideration of family dynamics. Each family member may agree to take on different responsibilities, which can work well. Or having one family member take the lead on all duties may be more effective.

For many, addressing final wishes is a most daunting task. There is much to consider, and uncomfortable emotions may add to feeling overwhelmed.

To draw up your legal documents, seek the help of an elder law attorney who can make the process less stressful and prepare essential documents such as a Durable Power of Attorney to designate an Attorney-in-fact for financial and business matters and a Medical Power of Attorney to designate a Health Care proxy. In addition, an attorney can explain the details, answer questions, and help with the distribution details regarding material possessions, property, and money.

When these documents are prepared and ready for signatures, review them word for word to ensure they reflect your family member's wishes. Review and update records as circumstances change, typically every three years. Why update? Life is fluid. For example, people come in and out of your life, and wishes can change due to the death of a close family member, family dynamics, financial and marital status, and losing touch with friends.

Inaccurate or out-of-date information discovered during the distribution of assets can cause devastating emotional and financial consequences for the beneficiaries.

It's common for people to postpone creating or updating their legal documents. Sadly, a family member can unexpectedly become incapacitated or die before completing their arrangements. Or they made their wishes known to a particular family member without officially updating their Will, leaving the family unable to fulfill their wishes.

In our family's case, Dad had contacted an attorney and completed documents according to his wishes. When he died unexpectedly in 1989, the distribution of his estate was easy for Mom and me. In addition, he kept labeled and organized files of investments, bank records, credit cards, monthly and annual expenses, and medical files. Finally, and most importantly, the wording in the legal documents gave Mom immediate access to cash in the bank and investment accounts. Mom and I were grateful for Dad's foresight and planning.

Let's explore why coordinating legal matters is important, why it may be difficult, and what steps you can take to prepare for a crisis.

Why Organizing Legal Matters Is Important

- ♥ When you initiate conversations to learn about your loved one's preferences, you plant seeds while you express love and willingness to help them fulfill their wishes.

- ♥ Having conversations and collecting and organizing essential documents makes you feel more in control and less stressed about the future.

- ♥ Enlisting the services of an Elder Law Attorney who you like, trust, and feel comfortable working with is essential. They will address your loved one's concerns and include all the critical information in the appropriate documents. The documents will be notarized and signed properly and you will have a complete record with all the information required.

- ♥ If designations for a Durable Power of Attorney and Durable Power of Attorney for Health Care are not made, critical decisions are left to third parties.

- ♥ Without a Last Will, estate distribution is placed into probate, with the family losing all control.

- ♥ No one can carry out an individual's wishes without accurate documentation.

- ♥ **Why is organizing legal matters important to you?**

Why Organizing Legal Matters May Be Difficult

- Conversations about aging and death may be uncomfortable. Discussing personal and private details when your family does not typically share this information requires patience and skill.

- You may not have faced your own fears surrounding these topics, and until you understand your thoughts, it can be challenging to engage your loved ones in a conversation about their wishes.

- Your wishes may differ from your loved one's wishes, and it may be difficult to respect and honor their preferences if you are conflicted and haven't had open communication to understand their choices.

- **Why is organizing legal matters difficult for you?**

ACTION PLAN: Organize Legal Matters

Using this checklist as a guide, begin to prepare for your conversation. When and with whom will you start the conversation? Communication is essential while family members are healthy and before a crisis or health deterioration. If you are already in a caregiving situation, NOW is the best time.

1. If your family member is not ready for this conversation, offer them a copy of the checklist. Request they gather the information in one place and inform you where they put it.

2. If documents already exist, find out how old they are, and note the contact information for the attorney. Find out if the attorney is still practicing or has changed location.

3. If documents already exist, but your loved one has moved from another state, married or dissolved a marriage, have your loved one consult an attorney immediately, as state laws vary, and new documents likely need to be prepared.

4. Ask your loved one who they designated Durable Power of Attorney, Durable Power of Attorney for Health Care, and Personal Representative. Ensure these individuals are still the people desired and the people named have been informed and agree to the responsibility.

5. Review the documents with your family member, and if needed, help them update the information and go with them to visit the attorney.

6. If you or your loved one dislikes their current attorney, do not hesitate to find a new one. Get recommendations from friends and find an attorney you trust who can guide you through this process and complete the required documents.

7. At a minimum, if your family member insists on privacy, request the attorney's contact information, and ask where they keep their important documents and who has a copy of them.

8. The checklist for arrangements

    a. A Will. Possibly a Trust.

    b. Durable Power of Attorney.

    c. Durable Power of Attorney for Health Care. It may also be called a Health Care Surrogate or Medical Power of Attorney.

d. Personal Representative or Executor of the Estate.

e. Specific instructions on leaving monetary and material possessions to people or distributing stuff while competent.

Please visit www.HOCToni.com/actionplan/
for a free download of this Action Plan.

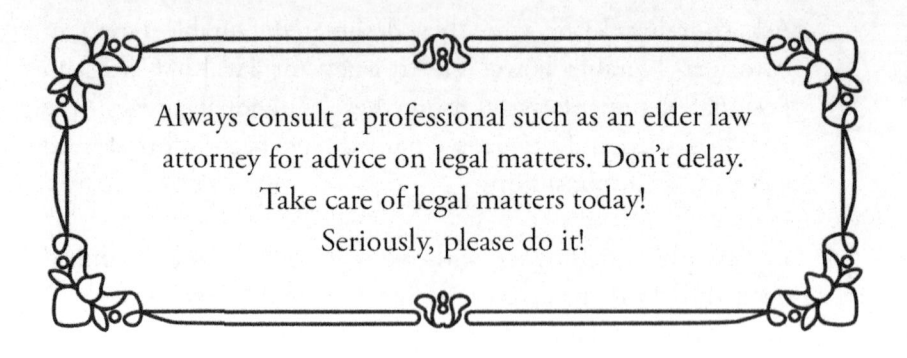

> Always consult a professional such as an elder law attorney for advice on legal matters. Don't delay. Take care of legal matters today!
> Seriously, please do it!

There are two different types of financial caregivers. The first is a caregiver who also provides financial support and contribution for their loved one. The average out-of-pocket expenses a caregiver pays on behalf of their loved one is $7,000 per year. (According to "Family Financial Caregiving: Rewards, Stresses and Responsibilities,": AARP, 2015) According to a Merrill Lynch study, 68 percent of caregivers report that they are financial contributors.
The second type of financial caregiver is the financial coordinator. This person manages the hands-on financial activities of paying bills, dealing with insurance, managing assets and investments, filing taxes and monitoring accounts. According to the same Merrill Lynch study, 88 percent of caregivers handle financial coordination tasks, and 64 percent of caregivers report that they are providing both financial coordination and financial support for the person receiving care.
—Sonya Edwards, Director of Financial Counseling at Empowering and Strengthening Ohio's People (a subsidiary of *Benjamin Rose Institute on Aging*)

MISTAKE # 17

NOT ASSESSING FINANCIAL INFORMATION

A crisis happens suddenly and without notice, and if financial affairs are not in order or there are limited funds, it can devastate a family. When assigned attorney-in-fact through a Durable Power of Attorney (DPOA), you can legally manage financial matters for your loved one, which stays in effect when they cannot do so themselves. For this reason, it is essential to establish POAs when your loved one is competent to assign responsibility and share their wishes. Ideally, every adult would designate an attorney-in-fact and maintain a Durable Power of Attorney in their legal documents.

You don't know all that you will encounter as your loved one ages, so financial needs are unpredictable, but you know that medical and long-term care in the United States are expensive. Issues related to aging and caregiving expenses are costly and increase regularly. If a family cannot afford the costs or their savings get depleted, this may impact your savings. Reports consistently estimate that out-of-pocket expenses for the caregiver can exceed $5,000 annually. In addition, some caregivers will utilize FLMA (Family Medical Leave Act) or eventually leave the financial security of their jobs altogether to provide required care.

Information about your loved one's financial assets will help you prepare for future medical costs, especially since health insurance policies often do not cover home care, respite care, and other expenses. Consider and explore long-term care policies. While they have limits and conditions and include a waiting period before benefits begin, they can significantly reduce future costs.

> Mom has been using the same financial planner and accountant for many years. They are familiar with Mom's assets and yearly tax responsibilities. I use them as well, which simplifies interactions. Mom is eager to have help managing her assets and having me manage her medical expenses. While Mom is healthy and living in her home, we make a spreadsheet of her monthly expenses vs. income. Then, we investigate assisted living facilities and compare those costs with her current living situation. When the time comes to consider moving Mom to an assisted living facility, we review the plan and agree it is an excellent option. By then, I need support, and Mom welcomes extra care and more social interaction.
>
> She lives there for eleven years—not something we imagined. The facility raises prices annually, which

I learn to question. When they reduce it by several percentage points, I wish I knew to negotiate sooner.

Let's explore why organizing financial affairs is important, why it may be difficult, and how you can begin to help your family member manage their financial affairs.

Why Assessing Financial Information Is Important

- ♥ You reduce worry and stress when your loved one's financial information is in order, and you are well-informed about account status and policy information.

- ♥ When you know your loved one's financial details, including passwords, you can help them make decisions regarding their future that fit within their budget.

- ♥ Where your loved one lives as they age is likely one of the most significant decisions they will make. Understanding their financial picture will enable you to partner with them on what matters most.

- ♥ Medical expenses can quickly deplete assets. If you are not current on a loved one's financial situation and they lose the capacity to manage their affairs, you may discover a critical situation too late.

- ♥ Your savings and financial position can be at risk if you become responsible for your loved one's bills and other payments.

- ♥ Keeping up with your loved one's accounts ensures that one of you pays the bills to avoid the costs of late or unpaid accounts.

♥ Care expenses may require you to leave the security of your job to provide needed care, which impacts your current income and retirement income, including social security.

♥ If your loved one does not name a Durable Power of Attorney, at the minimum, there will be a disruption of bank account access, access to manage investments, inability to pay bills, recurring expenses, and continuing medical needs and costs.

♥ **Why is assessing your loved one's financial information important to you?**

Why Assessing Financial Information May Be Difficult

- Financial information can be considered personal and private. Some people shy away from sharing this information with their children or other family members, making financial topics difficult to broach.

- Your loved one may view managing their financial affairs as a sign of independence, so by stepping in to help, you may challenge their dignity.

- Money can be a triggering subject, and financial conversations can cause anxiety. Sensitivity is required.

- **Why is assessing your loved one's financial information difficult for you?**

ACTION PLAN:
Assess Financial Information

1. Having financial conversations while family members are healthy and can participate is ideal before a crisis, or their health deteriorates. If you are already in a caregiving situation, NOW is the next best time to begin the discussions.

2. Decide with whom and when you will start the conversation to understand and help organize your loved one's financial information. Test the waters by asking simple questions like, "Where do you bank?" Set the stage for collaboration. Your objective is to be able to help your loved one if needed.

3. If the conversation moves forward, pick the areas to start now. Set a date for the follow-up conversation and information-gathering session so you can promptly fill in the Financial Checklist details.

4. Revisit this conversation until you know the information is accurate and complete.

5. Help your loved one create or organize an existing filing system that includes this information for easy access.

6. Use these checklists as guides. If your family member is not ready to have this conversation, offer them a copy of these checklists, request they gather this information in one place, and ask them to inform you where they keep it.

FINANCIAL PLANNING LIST

1. Current Fixed Expenses
2. Current Fixed Annual Expenses

3. Current Monthly Deductions

4. Current Fixed Income (all sources) – Monthly/quarterly/annually

FINANCIAL CHECKLIST

If your loved one cannot manage their financial information, this checklist of information will help you or the individual designated Durable Power of Attorney.

1. Automatic deposits and deductions from accounts

2. Automobile, truck, boat titles, or payoff information

3. Bank records include the name of the bank, account numbers, safety deposit boxes and keys, debit card information, and location of check books

4. Birth, Marriage, Divorce, and Name Change certificates

5. Business records

6. Change of Address, list of those to advise

7. Contact information for the financial advisor and accountant

8. Credit card information with most current statements

9. Debts, including Lines of Credit, Overdrafts, Mortgages

10. Deeds, Property Records, Titles

11. Medical Costs and Insurance

12. Income

13. Internet and account passwords

14. Investment accounts

15. Military records and VA benefits

16. Passport

17. Recurring Bills, including dates and method of payment

18. Savings Bonds

19. Social Security

20. Tax returns (at least one year)

21. Other

Please visit www.HOCToni.com/actionplan/ for a free download of this Action Plan.

> The financial decisions made or not made today will impact you and your loved one's future. You have options now that will narrow as time passes. Learn from professionals, make informed decisions, and know you have done everything possible to prepare for what's coming.

PART VII

DISMISSING HAPPINESS

Without love and kindness life is cold, selfish and uninteresting and leads to distaste for everything. With kindness, the difficult becomes easy, the obscure clear; life assumes a charm and its miseries are softened. If we knew the power of kindness, we should transform the world into a paradise.
—Charles Wagner, 1852-1918
French Reformed Pastor, Author

Life is meant to be a celebration!
It shouldn't be necessary to set aside
special times to remind us of this fact.
Wise is the person who finds a reason
to make every day a special one.
—Leo F. Buscaglia, American author, motivational speaker

MISTAKE # 18

NOT CELEBRATING WITH YOUR LOVED ONE

I agree with Leo Buscaglia. Life should be a celebration no matter what the circumstances. Bad things happen at one time or another, but dwelling on the bad is a form of self-inflicted suffering and can lead to more upset or even depression.

Each caregiving journey is unique. Whether your loved one is experiencing the effects of aging or progressive disease, you may encounter uncomfortable twists and turns, unexpected potholes, and circumstances that leave you inconsolable. While it's understandable to focus on the things that go wrong, and fear the future, to improve well-being, choose to focus on the good. Notice and celebrate the successes, what goes according to plan, and each day's accomplishments, no matter how small.

A good life consists of many joyous moments. Those moments, activities, and relationships become the memories you treasure.

What would it look like in your life to celebrate each day? Every morning, create an intention of celebrating. Focus on relationships and connecting more deeply with the people in your life.

While caring for Mom, I focus on two questions: What will be fun to do with Mom today? How can we celebrate being alive today? Life gets immediately better. Some days are low energy, and we sit together watching a tennis tournament on TV and eating our favorite ice cream. She knows the names of all the tennis players and has her favorites. From her recliner, she cheers for the exceptional points won and jeers at the referees when she thinks they make a bad call. I find real joy as I watch her get so excited. When we have more energy, we go out and get her hair done or go shopping.

Once, with a map of Orlando (where we live), noting restaurants, exhibits, and entertainment schedules, I diligently plan a trip to Epcot Center. I bring a paid caregiver to take the pressure and stress off me, so I can focus on enjoying the experience with Mom. The caregiver is in charge of pushing Mom in the wheelchair, taking her to the bathroom, and photographing all of us. Even though I help, I enjoy the excursion more with assistance. I will treasure the photographs from that day for the rest of my life.

I make a big deal about Mom's 95th birthday party. I hire a band, entertainment, and cater a dinner buffet with a beautifully decorated chocolate cake and chocolate-covered strawberries. We invite friends from near and far and the entire community at the assisted living facility—about 100 strong! It's all on video and photos, and I will love reliving the event. The residents say it is the best party they have ever attended and talk about it for months. They ask me if there will be a 100th birthday party. I respond, "Yes, likely, but there will also be a 96th, just in case."

I find ways to celebrate on some days when Mom doesn't feel very well. For example, Mom wakes up with a right-sided Bell's Palsy manifested by a drooping right side of her face. We are in the emergency room, where we have been so often, and it looks like we will be here for hours again.

Mom asks, "Am I going to die this time?"

I am familiar with her condition and assure her that she will not die but will need tests and likely have a long recovery. A minute later, I ask Mom, "If you were going to die, what's one story you would want me to tell others about your life?" I grab my notebook and pen and, for the next 30 minutes, document Mom's story about how she met and married her "Prince Charming."

Now that's turning lemons into lemonade, celebrating my parents and their life, and making good use of our time together. To date, hundreds of people have heard Mom's story!

You can include others in an activity or celebration, broaden your circle of friends, socialize, and have fun. Others may enjoy planning an event for or with you.

Let's explore why daily celebration is important, why it may be difficult, and how to create, capture, and make the most of those unique and memorable moments.

Why Celebrating Is Important

- ♥ Life is a series of moments. These moments pass without much distinction, and those that catch your attention become your treasured memories. First, they are memories for today to share again and again with your loved one. Second, these are memories for you, for tomorrow, memories that will stay with you after your loved one's passing.

- ♥ When you step out of the worry cycle, shift to a positive attitude, and explore how to celebrate each day, you enrich your life with beautiful experiences and create happy, meaningful memories.

- ♥ When you include others in your celebrations, big and small, it is a gift for your loved one, for you, and the people participating in the fun—a triple win!

- ♥ A positive attitude is contagious. Family and friends will be eager to spend time with you.

- ♥ Missed opportunities to create joy may cause you to regret not taking the time to appreciate and make the most of your time together.

- ♥ When you resist rather than accept your circumstances, you can feel hopeless and depressed. In this state, your life lacks purpose. Identifying ways to celebrate each day will give you purpose and inspire hope.

- ♥ **Why is celebrating daily important to you?**

Why Celebrating May Be Difficult

- Worry and uncertainty can overwhelm you, causing inaction, procrastination, and a lack of appreciation for the present moment.

- You may not be naturally positive and outgoing, so engaging with people may feel uncomfortable.

- Finding ways to celebrate might feel like an impossible and undesirable task if you are mired in negativity and resent your caregiver role and responsibilities.

- **Why is celebrating daily difficult for you?**

ACTION PLAN: Celebrate

1. Make today a celebration. What can you do today to celebrate your time with your loved one?

2. Remind yourself regularly to be in the present moment and decide to notice the good things happening in your life. You might set an hourly reminder to tune into your surroundings and look for something positive. The moments pass quickly, adding

to days, weeks, months, and years of missed opportunities if you don't act.

3. When a negative thought emerges, say "Thank you for sharing" or "Cancel!" and dismiss it with a wave of your hand.

4. Keep a gratitude journal. Write down three things you are grateful for every day—anything. Repetition is allowed. It can be a person, place, thing, or anything else. No limits to your imagination, no wrong answers. Daily gratitude journaling is proven to boost your happiness level. More happiness = more focus on celebrating.

5. Reflect and write down your successes or wins throughout the day. Share them with someone you love. Ask the other person to do the same.

6. When you are passionate about something, you become unstoppable. Become passionate about creating moments with your loved one to appreciate today and treasure tomorrow.

7. List what is not working in your life or the worries draining you of joy, happiness, and celebrating. Make it as extensive as you can. What is draining your energy in relationships, the environment, career, finances, home, and health?

    a. Identify the items that you cannot control. Set an intention to let go of them. Regularly review your progress.

    b. Identify the things in your control and take action toward resolving the issue. Change what you can change. What's the next step to resolve a worry? And the next step? And so on.

8. Get creative or ask a friend or family member to help you find ways to celebrate relationships, history, and family. Document

the small joys daily by photographing to record fun moments or journaling the highlights.

9. If you are overwhelmed with worry or sadness, ask for help. Reach out to a friend or professional and explore your feelings so that you can begin the shift to gratitude, joy, and abundance.

Please visit www.HOCToni.com/actionplan/
for a free download of this Action Plan.

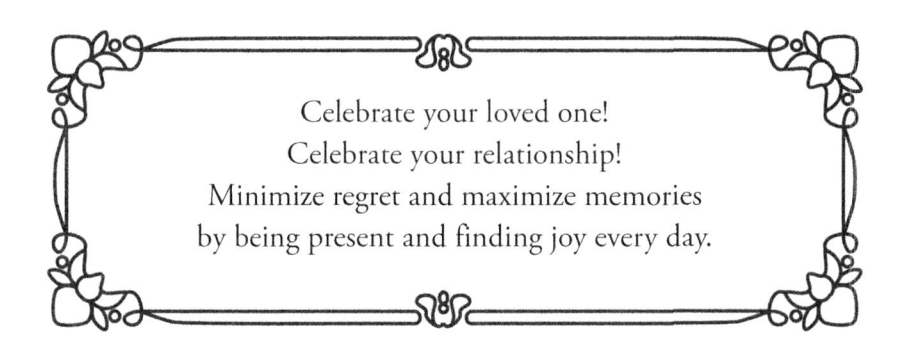

> Celebrate your loved one!
> Celebrate your relationship!
> Minimize regret and maximize memories
> by being present and finding joy every day.

You can't wait until life isn't hard anymore before you decide to be happy.
—Jane "Nightbirde" Marczewski, *America's Got Talent* Contestant, 2021; auditioned despite living with cancer in her lungs, spine, and liver. Died 2.19.22

MISTAKE # 19

PUTTING YOUR HAPPINESS ON HOLD

Caregiving and happiness can seem mutually exclusive when struggles and worry are all-consuming. You know caregiving is complex, with seemingly impossible challenges. Your negative thoughts and beliefs add to the suffering and pain, creating stress, worry, guilt, and arguments with family and friends. What if there is an alternative? What if you can find happiness while you face struggles? Otherwise, you put your happiness on hold, wait for life to be less stressful, and miss out on some of our best opportunities to experience joy. Even though you may be predisposed to happiness, with intention and strategy, you can be happy even during some of the most challenging circumstances.

I've been trying to understand happiness my whole life, starting when my very handsome high school sweetheart "dumped" me in favor of dating another woman. I am devastated. Mom recognizes my sadness when I walk into the house after the incident, and we have a brief conversation. Then, she leaves me with the following comment, "I just want you to be happy." I would feel better if she outlined at least five tips for happiness, but I'm on my own. I search in the self-help section of bookstores. I follow traditional advice to attend college, get a good job, and get married. While I have a good and mostly happy life, I learn there is much more to happiness.

Then, to my delight, in 2004, I discover the study of positive psychology, The Science of Happiness, when I contribute a chapter to a compilation book. Stephen J. Kraus, Ph.D., one of the other contributors, wrote about implementing recommended behaviors to increase happiness. In addition, I later learn that happiness is possible through intentional habit changes. Only 10% of happiness is due to external circumstances, and a surprising 90% to the internal environment. Therefore, we can all shift our happiness levels. How? Your intentional daily activities and choices influence a whopping 40% of your happiness.

You may use lack of choice to justify your unhappiness. For example, many of us don't choose to become caregivers. You may have taken responsibility due to love or obligation. You may be able to acknowledge that, given your decision, you have a choice about how you will let the experience affect you. So, you can learn and grow from each challenge and be grateful for new knowledge and skills. You can accept that while caregiving tests you, you can find new ways to take care of yourself to stay strong. These are examples of choices you can make. Likewise, you can choose to be happy and find happiness within the caregiving experience.

I intentionally look for activities to share with Mom that favor increasing our happiness. Since I love writing and want to end the day on a positive note, I suggest to Mom that we start a gratitude journal together. "What are you grateful for, Mom?" "You!" she says without hesitation. "What else? Two more." "I always wanted to be a mom, and I am so blessed that you are my daughter. Even though I am getting old and have many health issues, I am so happy to still be here and have more time with you." I get goosebumps and that good tingly feeling when she expresses her love to me.

My turn. I respond with my gratitudes. "Number one, I'm very grateful you are still in my life. I am grateful that you love me so much and express it often. And what else? Here's a good one. I'm grateful that you love playing poker with the men and that often you get excited because you win money!" We both have a good laugh about the poker games. Despite the circumstances, we end the day with laughter and good feelings.

By including an intentional practice for happiness in your daily living plan, you may find it to be fun and easy to implement and bring immediate relief. Sometimes, you may feel that your course is set and can't be changed when you experience sadness or exhaustion. Therefore, it's essential to remember that one small step at a time can help you make a significant change over time. Think baby steps.

Let's explore why focusing on happiness is important, why it may be difficult, and how you can invite more joy into your life.

Why Focusing On Happiness Is Important

- ♥ When you decide to be happy, your positive outlook on life will lead you to more happiness.

- ♥ People are drawn to be around happy people. You make more friends, and people will be more willing to help when you are joyful. Alternatively, when you constantly focus on the negative, family and others don't want to be around you, causing you to feel further isolated.

- ♥ Happiness is contagious; exuding joy positively affects others and will lift their spirits.

- ♥ You feel more in control of life.

- ♥ You feel stronger when choosing battles and discerning which ones are worthwhile.

- ♥ You experience more joy with your loved one and for the entire caregiving experience.

- ♥ You recognize and embrace opportunities to develop a deeper loving relationship with your loved one.

- ♥ **Why is focusing on happiness important to you?**

Why Focusing On Happiness May Be Difficult

- When you believe that you do not deserve happiness, your beliefs will undermine your efforts to be happy.

- You may believe that being happy and caregiving are mutually exclusive.

- There is a payoff when you identify as a victim of caregiving, so if you portray happiness, you would have to give up your victim status.

- Unhappiness might be your "default" state for various reasons.

- You are not present with your feelings of happiness when they occur, so you miss them.

- You miss the small miracles and the joyful moments because you are not looking for them.

- Caregiving becomes a duty to perform and separate from your life, so you are less engaged with the potential of the experience.

- **Why is focusing on happiness difficult for you?**

ACTION PLAN:
Focus On Happiness

---

1. Set an intention to be happy. Despite your feelings and circumstances, your caregiving experience can bring you and your loved one many moments of happiness.

2. Examine beliefs that undermine your intention to be happy. For example, why do you believe happiness is not possible? What is preventing you from being happy? What do you tell yourself?

3. Eliminate negative thoughts that interfere with allowing happiness.

4. Demonstrating curiosity about your loved one's life creates a deeper connection, which results in greater happiness. What is meaningful in their life? For example, their accomplishments? What have they learned? Ask probing questions and remember to listen. Be curious about those you encounter throughout the day. The receptionist at the doctor's office has a story. The person bagging your groceries has a story. Everyone appreciates

the opportunity to talk about themselves. Appreciate and thank them as well.

5. Look for the miracles or the big and small moments that inspire wonder in your daily life. Then, watch them multiply.

6. Focus on relationships with attention on the positive, what is good, what is working, what is right, and what is possible. Diminish your focus on past disappointments and regrets.

7. Make a concerted effort to trust that friends, family, health care professionals, and the "universe" are there to support you.

8. Each day, journal the positive events, successes, miracles, and marvels, and write down three things for which you are grateful.

9. Lead with a sweet disposition. Friendly is good! Smile at people. Showing warmth and kindness always wins over complaining, arguing, demanding, threatening, and whining.

10. Demonstrate vulnerability with an open heart by regularly expressing gratitude, generosity, kindness, and compassion toward everyone you meet. Being vulnerable may feel uncomfortable at first. Keep practicing.

11. Offer appreciation, approval, and acknowledgment. What do you like about the people you meet today, including your loved one? Tell them. It will lift their spirits. What have they done to enrich your life? Tell them.

12. Give the gift of attentive listening. There is grace when you show a genuine interest in another person and have an unhurried conversation to know and understand them at a level beyond the superficial. Ask a question. Be quiet. Listen intently to their answer until they finish talking.

13. Put on your dancing shoes. Have fun, laugh, and play. Life is an adventure. Invite people to "dance" with you. What can you do today for fun?

14. Let gratitude be your attitude. If you have yet to start that gratitude journal, today is a perfect time. Three gratitudes a day increases your energy, happiness, and positive outlook on life. What are your three gratitudes?

15. Develop an eye for miracles. The more you open your eyes to the blessing of life around you, the more you will enjoy the people in your life, the places you go, and the circumstances that confront you. Start by asking for what you need and noticing the response you get from anywhere and anyone.

16. Demonstrate loving honesty. Say "yes" when you mean "yes" and "no" when you mean "no." Don't be afraid to make promises to people. Ask for help when you need it and offer service when others need it. Set boundaries that support your self-care. Be truthful.

17. Practice "reception perception." Tune in to know when your listener has tuned out. Is the person listening when you are talking to them? Consider your words, your tone of voice, the volume of your voice, and the feelings behind the message you are delivering. Are you calm or agitated?

18. Cultivate resilience. Life is uncertain. Develop the ability to bounce back after a fall. Stop holding grudges against people who have "wronged you." Learn to shake it off and move on with forgiveness.

19. Practice makes perfect. This stuff works. When these actions become habits, your happiness increases.

20. Teaching new skills helps you perfect them. What happiness insights can you share with your loved one, family, and friends?

21. Don't deny your emotions if you are sad, concerned, or afraid. Feel the feelings and realize that hope, positivity, and happiness are all available to you.

Please visit www.HOCToni.com/actionplan/
for a free download of this Action Plan.

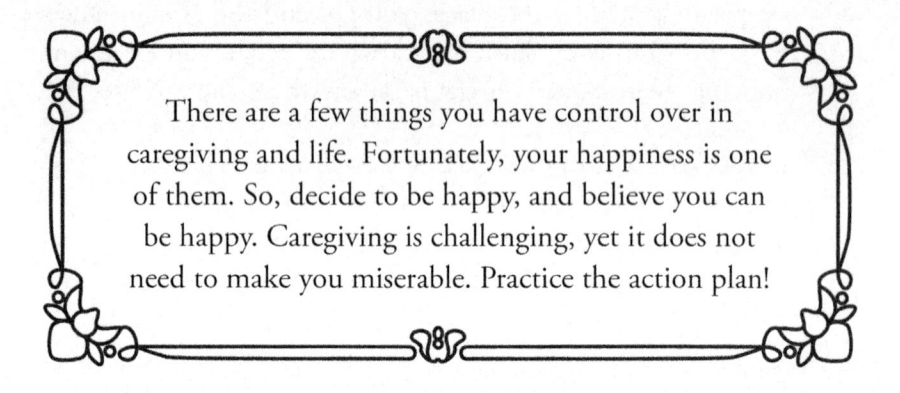

> There are a few things you have control over in caregiving and life. Fortunately, your happiness is one of them. So, decide to be happy, and believe you can be happy. Caregiving is challenging, yet it does not need to make you miserable. Practice the action plan!

Jewish mysticism says, every obstacle or what we call today, a "trigger," is really a boulder that can be transformed into a steppingstone towards incredible, profound depth, awareness, and spiritual greatness and we must seize those moments – so those moments that are making you crazy and really are bothering you, don't run from them, they are good places, there are a lot of hidden treasures there.
—Rabbi Yosef Yitzchak Jacobson, Chabad Rabbi and Teacher

MISTAKE # 20

ABANDONING YOUR RELIGIOUS OR SPIRITUAL PRACTICE

You may be firm in your commitment to your faith and practices if you have a strong belief system. Continue them for the hope and comfort they provide. However, if your loved one suffers a serious health crisis, you may disconnect or question your belief system and practices. Please reflect on your religious or spiritual journey and consider how your beliefs can influence and guide your caregiving experience.

With my mom, I had time to reflect on my beliefs about life, death, helping others, and my contribution to Mom and others. The eventuality of death triggered many questions when facing this reality with Mom. I suspect people often put off assessing matters until imminent illness or death faces them.

This exploration of religion and spirituality is a life-long journey for me. I was born into the Jewish faith but did not have a strong religious upbringing. After a comparative religion class in college, I discovered that the word "agnostic" described me best. In my 30s, spiritual courses I took captivated me. I began to understand the existence of a higher power and that there are many names associated with that power—God, Spirit, Universal Power, for example. The name doesn't matter.

Acknowledging this power's existence was a leap forward for me. During caregiving, I set aside this spiritual exploration and, looking back, see how I denied myself a critical component in my caregiver toolbox.

At the time of Mom's passing, I had been a caregiver for fourteen years, much longer than I initially expected. I found the conversations with the Hospice Chaplain (Mom liked the chaplain better than the rabbi!) enjoyable and calming. Today, I prioritize my spiritual connection and growth, which includes meditation, mindfulness, journaling, and spiritual guidance. These practices would have provided much-needed inner calm and peace of mind during my caregiving years.

Let's explore why staying connected to your spiritual self is important, why it may be difficult as caregiving intensifies, and how you can make time for this essential part of your experience.

Why Connecting To Your Religious Or Spiritual Practice Is Important

- ♥ The challenges of caregiving can deepen your understanding of yourself if you are willing to reflect and pray or mediate.

- ♥ You manage caregiving stressors and experience being calmer.

- ♥ You minimize self-doubt and increase your faith that people and the universe lovingly support you.

- ♥ You feel more connected with all of life and less lonely on your journey.

- ♥ You gain clarity of your purpose on earth.

- ♥ You increase your ability to ask for and receive guidance.

- ♥ You receive emotional grounding and the knowledge that you are not alone.

- ♥ You experience love at a time when love can feel elusive.

- ♥ You experience joy, comfort, and peace from consistent practice.

- ♥ You enjoy a greater connection and confidence in your intuition.

- ♥ **Why is staying connected to your religious or spiritual practice important to you?**

Why Connecting To Your Religious Or Spiritual Practice May Be Difficult

- Lack of time to thoroughly explore your beliefs and thoughts.

- You may be at a low point in life. Even though reconnecting with your spirituality and inner self might be helpful, you may feel abandoned.

- You feel lost and afraid, so it's a challenge to regain balance and feel grounded again.

- **Why is staying connected to your religious or spiritual practice difficult for you?**

ACTION PLAN:
Connect To Your Religious Or Spiritual Practice

1. If you engage with a faith community, reach out and seek support. There will likely be other caregivers who would appreciate the opportunity to receive and provide help.

2. Explore and identify your current beliefs concerning God or a higher power. What practices are a fit for you at this time in your life? For example, prayer, meditation, journaling, asking for guidance, or attending a house of worship?

3. How have your beliefs or practices changed as you have progressed on your caregiving journey?

4. To get grounded in your new experience, take a moment to reflect on how your new role and responsibilities have impacted your life. Keep in mind these steps to help you process change:

    a. The first step in change is becoming aware of your situation.

    b. The second step is acceptance of where you are.

    c. The third step is reflecting on your current beliefs.

    d. The fourth step is taking action.

5. Consider a new practice, routine, or even deeper personal reflection to help you achieve the inner peace you desire. When you are overwhelmed, continually stressed, or must make a difficult decision, you may choose prayer, talking to your soul or spiritual mentors, or checking in with your intuition. Those moments making you crazy and bothering you may be trying

to teach you something important. Stop and listen. Tap into your heart and your guidance system.

6. If the concept of spiritual practice is new, consider studying a specific belief system that calls to you. Explore books, online websites, podcasts, workshops, group or personal coaching, audio tapes, and video learning, or consult a religious or spiritual counselor.

7. What have you learned from your loved one about their faith and practices, and how can you assist your loved one in implementing them?

8. Who can support you or share your spiritual journey?

> Please visit www.HOCToni.com/actionplan/
> for a free download of this Action Plan.

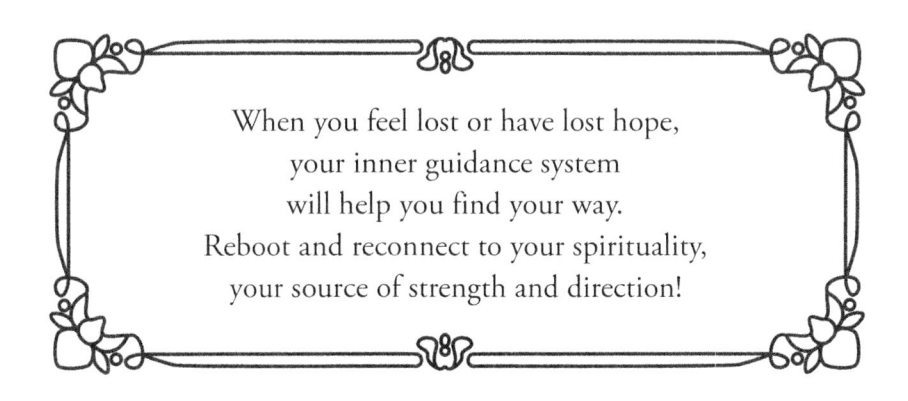

> When you feel lost or have lost hope,
> your inner guidance system
> will help you find your way.
> Reboot and reconnect to your spirituality,
> your source of strength and direction!

Perhaps the toughest battles in caregiving begin within.
Most battles really are about whether you are loved—
by your care recipient, by other family members, by friends,
by your significant other. End the battle now:
Know you have the love. Know it now so you can remind yourself later.
—Denise M. Brown, Caregiver
Founder, The Caregiving Years Training Academy

MISTAKE # 21

UNDERVALUING LOVE IN THE RELATIONSHIP

Everything you do for or say to your loved one is about loving them during this difficult time. The more love you give, the more love you receive. This time in your life may be the greatest joy in being alive, and if you see it as such, you will treasure the time with your loved one and the memories you make, and you will hold their love in your heart forever.

If you are caring for a parent, you have an opportunity to grow beyond your earlier dynamic that was perhaps "troubled," non-existent, or an immature love relationship. Compared to when you were younger, much is possible as open, non-judgmental, caring adults. A similar opportunity for growth and deeper intimacy is available when caring for your spouse or partner.

> I ask Mom questions about her life and understand her choices, hopes, and dreams, which deepens our connection. Coming from a place of expressing love while doing activities changes the experience and transforms caregiving chores. Acting

with loving intent, I approach caring for Mom as if it is a daily act of love, bringing joy to us both.

At first, it is not easy—daily to-do lists, managing multiple responsibilities and relationships, and caring for my needs and Mom. Emotional roller coaster. Lack of support and understanding from family and friends. Sleep deprivation. Stress, struggle, overwhelm. When will it end?

It is another day, another visit. I arrive at Mom's apartment even though my resentment is overpowering. I am in such a foul mood. While I hate the feeling, I can't shake it. I finally realize that my continuous caregiving duties are exhausting me. Even though Mom is in an assisted living community, I feel like a 24/7 caregiver. I respond to all her requests for company, errands, and needs. I don't want to say anything to Mom for fear of upsetting her. I enter Mom's apartment. As usual, she is sitting comfortably in her lift chair watching TV. Jasmine, our 7-pound, snow-white Maltese, makes a B-line over to Mom and jumps in her lap. Mom greets Jasmine, as always, with hugs and kisses and "lovey" noises.

Then, it hits me—one of the biggest ah-ha moments ever. My internal dialogue shouts, "I NEED THAT! THAT'S WHAT'S MISSING!" My dog is getting more love than I am. Now that I know what to ask for, I feel immediate relief. I have no idea what possesses me to get down on the floor on my hands and knees, but I do. Then I crawl awkwardly across the small living area to Mom. Mom stops loving on Jasmine and tilts her head, watching with increasing curiosity. Then, I stop in front of her chair, sit down, look up, and beg, "Mommy, pet me! Pet me, mommy, please!"

I feel her hand on my head, stroking lovingly. I need to be touched, and I need affection. She gives me what I need, and from that moment on, I can talk candidly about my feelings, and our relationship becomes more of a partnership. I give to mom, and she receives. Mom gives to me, and I receive. And LOVE is present because we learn to pay attention and focus on each other.

Let's explore experiencing more love and caring in your relationship, why it may be difficult to focus on love, and the steps to keep love at the forefront of your journey.

Why Expressing Love Is Important

- ♥ When you care for a loved one, you are in a close relationship and can both feel lonely. Your caregiving, care receiver, or care partner relationship provides a tremendous opportunity to experience love on a deeper level and have more love in your life.

- ♥ Expressing and receiving love gives you a more positive outlook on life, resulting in greater happiness.

- ♥ In the absence of giving and receiving love, negative emotions surface or simmer beneath the surface, not getting expressed, causing guilt and perhaps an illness. It could be resentment, anger, a reaction to your loss of freedom, or feeling obligated to help as there is no one else. Connecting with why you are caring for your family member and reconnecting with love in your relationship can reduce resentment and help you find meaning and purpose in your caregiving role.

- ♥ When you cultivate love in your relationship, your renewed purpose and meaning lead to greater happiness.

- ♥ **Why is expressing love important to you?**

Why Expressing Love May Be Difficult

- You never know how your actions or "love advances" will be received.

- Since we have become human-doing machines, it may be difficult to change behavior or mindset. Check in with yourself to notice if you are constantly *doing* things (essential as they are) but avoiding genuine connection and intimacy.

- Success is often measured by how much we get done in a day. As a caregiver, you prioritize getting things done, making and going to appointments, carrying out doctors' orders, handling insurance issues, seeking better medical care, planning activities, and solving problems to achieve better health and good quality of life for your loved one. Your list can feel endless, and taking time to show and receive affection can feel like another to-do on the list.

- Focusing *only* on being a doing machine will lead to burnout. Giving and receiving love may be difficult when you are burned out and numb from exhaustion and overwhelmed.

- **Why is expressing love difficult for you?**

ACTION PLAN:
Express Love

---

1. Making a concerted and intentional effort to love yourself and others. Each morning, decide that giving and receiving love is a priority and approach caregiving as an act of love. Ask yourself:

    a. How can I experience love with the person I am caring for?

    b. How can I give and receive love today?

2. Focusing on your errands and caregiving tasks as acts of love.

3. Taking time to connect physically with your loved one. What is appealing to that individual? Holding hands, a shoulder or back rub, sharing a hug, sitting close together on the sofa, a pet

on your lap, or even a toy animal or baby doll is comforting. Even if they cannot respond lovingly in a manner that rekindles your spirit, believe that your gesture does matter.

4. Exchanging gifts. I loved buying Mom small presents. They were always unexpected and brightened her day. I used online catalogs and would browse store aisles for fun finds. Organize your Care Community™ to come up with a creative project. Suggest ideas that would make your loved one happy.

5. Spending quality focused time. Mom and I usually took photographs to record our time together and revisit the experience at any time in the future.

6. A short video or audio message where the individual can see your face and hear the inflections in your voice will make your words even more powerful. Remember phone calls. They can be short check-in calls or long leisurely conversations. Greeting cards and letters sent through the postal mail usually bring a smile, can be displayed in your loved one's room and are treasured reminders of your love.

7. Remember to express your love, caring, and appreciation in person with your loved one. Even short in-person visits are appreciated and will lift their spirits.

8. In your gratitude journal, write down the people who make a positive difference. You might also send them a letter (an actual letter that you put in the mail) letting them know how much they mean to you.

Please visit www.HOCToni.com/actionplan/
for a free download of this Action Plan.

Forgiving and finding ways to express LOVE.
To love and be loved has been called a universal need.
With strained relationships, forgive yourself or your loved one
as needed and clear the path for love to show up.
Consider the opportunity that caregiving affords to live a
life of purpose and to provide meaningful connections.
Love is the greatest gift you give or receive.
Give love lavishly! Receive love abundantly!

Love is what we were born with. Fear is what we have learned here. The spiritual journey is the relinquishment—or unlearning—of fear and the acceptance of love back into our hearts. Love is the essential existential fact. It is our ultimate reality and our purpose on earth. To be consciously aware of it, to experience love in ourselves, and others, is the meaning of life.
—Marianne Williamson, Author, *Return to Love*

You've worked hard to get to where you are.
You've shown yourself that you are strong enough to handle
your challenges, even when you thought you couldn't.
You've experienced similar circumstances over and over again,
and your response to it has changed, showing your Super Power:
To be able to adapt, find wisdom for solutions,
and courage to keep on keeping on.
#projecthappiness

BEYOND MISTAKES – REFLECTIONS

Writing this book for you has given me substantial time to reflect on my caregiving experience, love for my mom, and lessons learned.

I highlight my stress, exhaustion, and unhealthy habits during my caregiving years because I discovered that experience is common. Nevertheless, I am proud of how I cared for Mom, and given what I know now, I understand more about how to support current and future family caregivers.

The people my mom and I met—professionals, other caregivers, and their parents—all impacted my growth and development and the quality of my life. Mom and I had good times together while I advocated for her health care and provided the best quality of life possible for her final years. I will always treasure the celebrations and joyful moments we shared.

I learned some incredible lessons about myself. I never considered myself an advocate until there was a crisis with Mom, and then I rose to the occasion. I found the strength to speak up to professionals and persist in finding the answers to health issues and treatments. I also learned to be kind, generous, and respectful of the nurses and assistants' time, who were so helpful in Mom's care.

I owe a lot to my mom and our caregiving experience. I gained confidence interacting with people. Caregiving has positively changed who I am. I am more patient with people and realize I never really know what challenges they face. I'm much less judgmental. Some people see me today as an extrovert, and after everything, I am grateful this caregiving experience did bring out my expressive and fun self.

YOUR 21 SUPER POWERS FOR CAREGIVING

1. You identify with the word "Caregiver."

2. You and your loved one have completed an "In-Case-of-Emergency" Go Bag (ICE) and plan with a notebook of medical information.

3. You understand how your caregiving journey may be the most impactful gift of your life, and treat yourself and your loved ones with care and compassion.

4. You recognize and accept when you notice a change in a family member's abilities.

5. When your loved one receives a diagnosis, you have a plan to address the situation and express emotions.

6. You know how to prepare, consider the options, and act within a reasonable timeframe to make difficult decisions.

7. You understand how your beliefs and attitudes can positively impact your caregiving experience.

8. You are beginning to understand your responsibilities as a caregiver.

9. You understand that when you care for someone, they depend on you as an advocate.

10. You put your health as a top priority and add people to your Care Community™ who support your mental, emotional, intellectual, and spiritual well-being.

11. You understand you cannot do every caregiving task and ask for help.

12. You know how to research a diagnosis and find local and national resources to support you and your loved one.

13. You know how to communicate effectively with your loved one and consider their needs, desires, and wishes.

14. You know how to communicate effectively with your family and friends to find out how they can help.

15. You know how to communicate effectively with physicians so they answer your questions, and you understand the care plan.

16. You are well-informed about the legal matters for someone you expect to care for in the future or who is currently under your care.

17. You are well-informed about the financial business of someone you expect to care for in the future or who is currently under your care.

18. Even during illness and the potential decline of your loved one, you cherish every moment with them and celebrate being together.

19. You practice the happiness principles each day.

20. You continue your religious or spiritual routine and activities.

21. You focus on receiving and expressing love.

Please visit www.hoctoni.com/actionplan/
for a free download of Caregiving Super Powers.

RESOURCES

TO GET YOU STARTED

National Organizations

Alzheimer's Association
www.alz.org
American Association of Retired People
www.aarp.org
www.aarp.org/preparetocare
American Cancer Society
www.cancer.org
American Heart Association
www.heart.org
Caregiver Action Network
www.caregiveraction.org
Department of Veteran's Affairs
www.va.gov
Disabled American Veterans
www.dva.org
Meals on Wheels America
www.mealsonwheelsamerica.org
National Academy of Elder Law Attorneys
www.naela.org
National Resource Directory
www.nrd.gov/resources
Today's Caregiver Magazine
www.caregiver.com

Specialty Organizations

Elite Cruises and Vacations Travel
www.elitecruisesandvacationstravel.com
Nana's Books Foundation
www.NanasBooks.org

The Care Years Training Academy
www.thecareyearstrainingacademy.com
The Five Wishes
www.agingwithdignity.org

Caregiving Agencies
Aging Care
www.agingcare.com
Area Agency on Aging
www.eldercare.acl.gov
Family Caregiver Alliance
www.caregiver.org
National Alliance for Caregiving
www.caregiving.org
Rosalynn Carter Institute for Caregivers
www.rosalynncarter.org/

Caregiving Consultants
Alison Van Schie
www.alongsidecaregiving.ca/podcasts-media
Certified Caregiving Consultant™
www.careyearsacademy.com/meet/
Elizabeth Miller
www.happyhealthycaregiver.com
Tanya Straker
www.tanyastraker.com
Theresa Wilbanks
www.SustainableCaregiving.com
Toni Gitles, Consultant, Educator
www.HeartofCaregiving.com

APPENDICES

APPENDIX 1

In-Case-Of-Emergency Go Bag

ACTION PLAN: Minimum to include in an In-Case-of-Emergency Go Bag (ICE) for your loved one

Medication List and Pertinent Information: 3 copies

1. Name of medication, dosage, when taken, what it is for, and the name and contact information of the doctor who prescribed it. (Identifying marks on the pill, and the shape, if possible, although this changes regularly with generic drugs). Add a start date for each medication.

2. Known allergies to medication. Medication name and description of the reaction. For example, I have a neurological autoimmune disorder called ocular myasthenia gravis. The disease comes with an extensive list of "cautionary medications" that can worsen my condition or kill me. I always carry a copy of this list. In addition, there are cautions for the anesthesiologist should I need surgery.

3. Name, address, and phone number of the pharmacy.

4. COVID-19 Vaccination history. Date of last negative test.

Health summary pages: 3-7 copies
Combine with the medication list

1. Illness, by date.

2. Past hospitalizations, surgical procedures, attending physician, and diagnoses by date. Include the hospital name and city if known.

3. Document dates of any out-of-country travel and resulting illnesses within the last six months.

Insurance and Personal Information

1. Driver's license or ID card—a copy of both sides.

2. Insurance cards—a copy of both sides.

Legal Documents

1. Designation of Health Care Surrogate—someone authorized to make medical decisions if the patient becomes incapacitated.

2. Do-Not-Resuscitate Orders (DNR), depending on the wishes of the loved one.

Contacts

Add other contacts and update as you access additional resources.

1. All current physicians and health care providers. Name and phone (minimum), address, email, practice name, therapists, home care agencies, and individuals providing paid help.

2. Add your name and contact information as the primary caregiver.

3. Family and friends—contact information.

Non-medical items for ICE Go Bag

1. Incontinence pads or briefs.

2. Extra pair of underpants, regular pants.

3. Extra pair of eyeglasses (in eyeglass case) or contacts.

4. Toothbrush, toothpaste, hairbrush, and items for dentures.

5. 48-hour supply of current medications (the pharmacy often substitutes medication).

NOTE: Other Documents

Not necessary for the hospital—helpful for you.

1. Know the location of health and life insurance policies, the long-term care policy, prepaid funeral contracts, and last wishes.

2. Social Security number in a secure location.

ACTION PLAN:
An Emergency Room Caregiver Bag

It's Not Uncommon To Be In The ER For 4 To 10 Hours. Why Not Have At Least The Minimum "Comfort" Items?

1. Your cell phone and cell phone charger (minimum 20 ft).

2. Water bottles or drinks.

3. Jacket. (Emergency rooms are generally cold!)

4. Snacks such as granola or nut bars, fruit, gum, or mints.

5. Wipes or napkins.

6. Notebook and pen (for notes, journal, or other uses).

7. Current reading material.

8. Copy of loved one's health insurance info, ID, or Driver's License, and people to notify.

9. Your emergency, family, and friend contacts.

10. Change of clothes.

11. Hairbrush, toothbrush, and toothpaste.

12. 48-hour supply of your medications.

13. Other items to consider are essential oils, devotional reading material, change for the vending machines, and a disabled person parking placard.

14. Add your items to the list—you might be there for hours and hours.

> Please visit www.HOCToni.com/actionplan/
> for a free download of Appendix 1.

APPENDIX 2

Journaling

- Buy two journals, one for you to document your caregiving journey and the other to document your loved one's health condition, doctor visits, recommendations, and treatments.

- You will write in the journal daily or as needed.

- Writing your thoughts and emotions down helps reduce stress and improve your mood.

- Putting your experience into words helps you organize your thoughts and feelings and gain clarity over your experiences rather than ignoring them.

- Writing each day about three things you are grateful for will increase your happiness.

- Writing about three positive things you experienced each day can reveal that the day wasn't as bad as it might seem.

- Monthly reviews of your journal about your life journey during caregiving can show you how far you've come and remind you of events, experiences, or feelings.

Please visit www.HOCToni.com/actionplan/ for a free download of Appendix 2.

APPENDIX 3

The Six Stages Of Caregiving

From: *The Caregiving Years, Your Guide to Navigating the Six Caregiving Stages* by Denise M. Brown
Ninth Edition, Copyright © 2021
The Caregiving Years Training Academy and Denise M. Brown
Excerpt with permission from the author

Stage I – The Expectant Caregiver

You have a growing concern that, within the near future, your family member or friend will need more and more of your assistance and time. You're concerned because of your relative's age, past and present medical condition, and current living condition.

Your Challenge

To learn and understand your caree's (the person you are caring for) needs: health, financial, legal, and emotional.

Your Purpose

You expect to become a caregiver; this is your time to prepare. You can research options, gather information, and provide the opportunity for your caree to share his or her feelings and values. This is also your time to concentrate on taking care of yourself—keeping up with family and friends, enjoying your hobbies and interests, pursuing your career goals.

Stage II – The Freshman Caregiver
You've begun to help your family member on a regular basis, weekly, perhaps even a few times a week. Your duties range from errand-running and bill-paying to some assistance with hands-on care.

Your Challenge
To discover solutions that work and to feel comfortable moving on from what doesn't.

Your Purpose
This is your entry into the caregiving role. This is your time to experiment, to get your feet wet and see what works. This is your opportunity to learn how the health care industry works with, or in some cases against, you. Now is the time to shape your caregiving personality: What duties are you comfortable with? What duties make you uncomfortable? How well are you and your caree getting along? What situations would create overwhelming stresses for both of you?

This is also the time when you get a feel for the present and future budgets needed to provide the care your caree requires.

In addition, keep up with your hobbies and interests (you may be able only to keep the ones that you enjoy most), ensuring you have made a habit of spending time on your own, enjoying yourself.

Stage III – The Entrenched Caregiver
Your involvement with your caree is almost daily—if not constant. Your caree may live with you—or your involvement means that your day is structured to be available to your caree. You begin to wonder, how much longer can you live this way? Your mood is sometimes upbeat—you're proud you've been able to provide such wonderful care and make decisions that support your caree's best wishes. Sometimes you feel melancholy—why you? You've been mourning

the loss of your caree's abilities and functions and often long for the days before caregiving. And, you're tired.

Your Challenge
To find the support and strength to continue.

Your Purpose
To develop a routine, create a familiar schedule for both yourself and your caree. A routine will help you deal with the overwhelming stresses and responsibilities that wear you out. A routine will provide comfort for you and your caree—this stage may be the most difficult for both of you. The changes you prepared for in Stage I and II are now a reality—you have become a lifeline to a family member or friend.

In addition to your caree's routine of care, create a routine for yourself. In your routine include time to manage the unexpected that pops up in your day; a ritual which begins and ends your day; and a "healthness" activity to nurtures your spiritual, emotional, physical, and mental needs.

Stage IV – The Pragmatic Caregiver
You've been through it all: hospital admission and discharges; short-term rehab stays in nursing homes; a vast array of community services. You've just been through the healthcare system long enough to know that you know your caree's needs best.

You also get the importance of a good laugh. Some family members and health care professionals may wonder about your ability to find humor in situations they find odd. You have a very practical, very realistic approach toward your caregiving role and your sense of humor has been a critical tool for your survival. Without your sense of humor, you would have given up a long time ago.

Your Challenge
To gain a greater understanding of yourself and your caree.

Your Purpose
To gain a better understanding of yourself and your caree. You've settled into your role and your routine; now is your opportunity to step back and reflect. The first three stages laid the groundwork for this stage, your period of personal growth.

Stage V – The Transitioning Caregiver
You've been caring for a period of time and now can sense the end.

Your Challenge
To let go of the fear of the end, to understand that reaching the end isn't about your failure but about the natural cycle of life. Now, you'll move from the "doing" of caregiving to focus on the "being." You're used to doing and going. It's time now to make being with your caree the priority.

Your Purpose
To walk with your caree during his last months and weeks, implementing his or her decisions about end-of-life care that you both discussed during Stage I (or as soon as you could). You can focus on loving and feeling good about the shared journey. As you both feel the journey end, this is also a time to mourn and grieve. You also will begin to question and worry about your life's next chapter.

Stage VI – The Godspeed Caregiver
Your role as caregiver ended more than two years ago. You find yourself compelled to make a difference in the lives of other caregivers. You share information readily with caregivers in the earlier stages. Perhaps you start a business dedicated to helping family caregivers or you find a job in which you assist family caregivers. Maybe you just make it a habit to smile at everyone because you know you could be smiling

at a family caregiver in need. You treasure each relationship you have in your life, recognizing that each day and your good health should never be taken for granted.

Your Challenge
To integrate your former role as a family caregiver into your new life.

Your Purpose
To implement your lessons learned from your role as caregiver, from your caree and from your family members and friends. During this stage, which can last as long you wish, even your lifetime, you reap the benefits of your efforts.

Please visit www.HOCToni.com/actionplan/
for a free download of Appendix 3.

APPENDIX 4

The Health Insurance Portability and Accountability Act of 1996 (HIPAA)

HIPAA is the acronym for the Health Insurance Portability and Accountability Act, passed by the U.S. Congress in 1996. HIPAA does the following:

- Provides the ability to transfer and continue health insurance coverage for millions of American workers and their families when they change or lose their jobs

- Reduces health care fraud and abuse

- Mandates industry-wide standards for medical information on electronic billing and other processes

- Requires the protection and confidential handling of protected health information and protects sensitive patient health information from being disclosed without the patient's consent or knowledge

- Includes The Privacy Rule that contains standards for individuals' rights to understand and control how their health information is used. A major goal of the Privacy Rule is to make sure that individuals' health information is properly protected while allowing the flow of health information needed to provide and promote high-quality medical care and protect the public's health and well-being. The Privacy Rule permits important uses of information while protecting the privacy of people who seek care and healing.

Please visit www.HOCToni.com/actionplan/ for a free download of Appendix 4.

APPENDIX 5

Action Plan For Building Your Care Community™

Create your Care Community™ and invite people in with a specific role. Let the people on your list know how much you appreciate them and how they help and support you.

You will be amazed at the number of people available to be on your list (don't disqualify anyone before a conversation). Document each person's name, phone, and email. Eventually, fill in how they help. Leave blanks to fill in later.

IDENTIFY PEOPLE IN YOUR CARE COMMUNITY™

Professionals

1. Physicians who care for your loved one and who care for you.

2. The nurses, office managers, receptionists, and surgery schedulers in the physicians' offices who you see regularly. Get to know them and their names. Be respectful and kind at every encounter.

3. Physical, occupational, and speech therapists.

4. Home health nurses, aides, and paid caregivers.

5. Names of specific care providers such as home care companies, home health care providers, assistive device suppliers, Certified Caregiving Consultants™, Care Managers, and Aging in Place Specialists.

6. People and organizations that provide education regarding caregiving and information on the illness or disease of your loved one—in person or virtual.

7. Accountant, financial advisor, and attorney.

Family and Friends

1. Family members—consider everyone, even those who live out of town. They can always call you and your loved one regularly to provide connection and support.

2. Best friends of yours and friends of your loved one, especially those who have been caregivers.

3. Leaders and volunteers from faith-based communities.

4. Your pet.

5. Neighbors.

6. Coworkers—current and previous.

7. People in any of your communities where you study, gather, or do charitable work.

8. Caregivers you meet in support groups, online caregiving groups, or on other social media.

9. Friends on social media.

10. Travel groups, investment groups, charitable groups you support, or other special interest groups.

IDENTIFY HOW FAMILY, FRIENDS, AND OTHERS CAN SUPPORT YOU AND YOUR LOVED ONE

How people help you or your loved one (or both) depend on whether you live together or in separate residences.

For you or your loved one:

1. Cleans the house, mows the lawn, fixes things that break around the house.

2. Occasionally cooks a meal or drops off groceries.

3. Helps financially.

4. Picks up medications.

5. Sends a cheerful greeting card on occasion.

6. Has a key to the house for emergencies.

7. Takes in the mail if needed.

8. Can gift a massage or dinner out.

For you, someone who:

1. Meets you at a restaurant for company, conversation, and a meal to give you a break from caregiving.

2. Always makes you laugh.

3. Is a good listener and will let you talk or vent without judgment.

4. Usually offers good advice.

5. You trust unconditionally.

6. Can be your accountability partner.

7. Mentors you in caregiving because they have been on a similar journey.

8. Is your backup for your loved one if **you** need to go to the emergency room or have a hospital stay.

9. Provides you with respite.

10. Does research on the internet or call local agencies and professionals to learn how they can help.

11. Gifts you a massage or spa visit.

12. Calls once a week to check how you are doing.

13. Helps you take your car for a service appointment.

14. Takes care of your plants if needed.

15. Cares for your pet at your home or theirs (may include appointments with the vet or groomer).

16. Will discuss spiritual or religious beliefs or practices.

17. Can help you talk through your emotions and especially depression.

For your loved one, someone who:

1. Visits your loved one without you there.

2. Takes them to a doctor's appointment or meets you there for support.

3. Takes care of your loved if **you** need to go to the emergency room or have a hospital stay.

4. Can take on visits with them when in hospital or rehab.

5. Can be a companion to provide social interaction for 30 minutes, an hour, or more. Even a short visit is appreciated.

6. Can loan a walker, wheelchair, shower chair, or bedside portable toilet.

7. Helps with bathing, dressing, feeding,

This list is your caregiving plan and **your Lifeline** and will serve you well, especially if your caregiving lasts years instead of weeks or months. Recognize that sometimes the same person can serve in multiple capacities! Feel free to add your support categories to this list, which can become a spreadsheet you can readily access.

Please visit www.HOCToni.com/actionplan/
for a free download of Appendix 5.

APPENDIX 6

Guidelines for Effective Conversations (It helps if you agree on certain things from the start)

Open and honest communication is key to any relationship. Outstanding communication skills will change your life for the better. You cannot control what the other person says. However, you can control whether you react or respond and what you say. People who are the most difficult to deal with are the ones who need your love and acceptance the most.

- ♥ Think of the relationship as a partnership and get curious about what your loved one wants and needs.

- ♥ To encourage your loved one to value your help, stay calm, don't take anything personally, be patient, and ask specific questions to start the conversation or further your understanding of their wants and needs.

- ♥ Make every effort to avoid interrupting your loved one while they are still expressing their opinion. Interrupting and making assumptions about what your loved one wants and needs can create conflict and sidetrack your main goal.

- ♥ Listen with the intent of asking questions and getting clarification.

- ♥ Find out how your loved one feels.

- ♥ If they are a person of few words, accept that they have said all there is to say or learn to ask a question about "today."

  - How can we best spend our time together?

  - What do we need help with?

  - How can we assist each other?

  - How can we give and receive love?

  - How can we laugh and have fun?

  - What's one thing I can do for you to make your day better?

  - What do you need?

  - What are your concerns?

  - How does that make you feel?

- ♥ Give your loved one your complete attention rather than multi-tasking!

- ♥ Speak from your heart and be honest. Be kind, considerate, and loving. Practice gratitude and kindness.

- ♥ Allow silence. People need time to answer a question or formulate what and how they want to say something.

- ♥ Avoid getting defensive and arguing for your position. Avoid blame, judgment, or criticism.

- ♥ Keep your voice calm and avoid making demands or insisting they do things your way.

- Don't allow your feathers to get ruffled over differing viewpoints. Fully hear your loved one and listen until they finish talking.

- Let go of the past.

- If you think they have finished talking or stating their opinion, ask, "Is there anything else you'd like to add?" Repeat your question until they say there is nothing else.

- Now it's your turn to give your opinion (with reasons) or feelings about the issue and respond to what they have said, pointing out their positive ideas.

- Identify your points of agreement.

- Always be kind and say, "Thank you for having this conversation with me. It was truly helpful."

Please visit www.HOCToni.com/actionplan/
for a free download of Appendix 6.

APPENDIX 7

Preparation For A Doctor Visit

You already have taken responsibility for helping your loved one. The physician will appreciate the preparation and get you the best information on care. It takes the stress out of the appointment and wondering what to report.

1. Before an office visit, have your loved one document (or you help them) relevant information to report since the previous visit. Include relevant symptoms, when they started, how long they have occurred, and any medication changes and hospitalization history. Keeping a journal will facilitate having this information readily available, and you won't have to count on your memory.

2. Prior to an office visit, ask your loved one what they would like to tell the doctor and what they would like to know by the end of the visit. Know the purpose of the visit and what information you need from the doctor.

3. Prepare any questions you can think of beforehand and listen closely when the doctor is talking so you can ask additional questions as needed.

4. Whether this is a first or follow-up visit in the emergency room, hospital, or physician's office, when communicating with health care professionals, present a thorough history of health concerns. Be specific, mention all symptoms,

and always get to the point rather than give an extensive play-by-play story.

Please visit www.HOCToni.com/actionplan/
for a free download of Appendix 7.

APPENDIX 8

Why You Don't Ask For Help

Most caregivers face and typically avoid asking for help. You *COULD* ask for help right now, but there are so many reasons you don't.

1. Identify and give up thoughts or beliefs that prevent you from asking for help. You may think, "People don't want to be bothered," or "People will feel obligated and resentful if I ask them for help."

2. Practice delegating, even though it seems easier to do it yourself.

3. You may see asking for help as a character flaw, believing, "I should be able to do this without help" or "I'm weak if I can't do this alone."

4. You may think no one will help, and you dislike anyone rejecting you. When someone responds "no" to your request, give them the freedom to do so without getting dramatic or angry.

5. You've asked before, and the people didn't do what they said they would, interfering with your plans and upsetting you. Since you had to do it yourself anyway, why bother asking again?

See yourself in there?? Great!! NOW—Let it go! Your beliefs are interfering with the results you desire. It doesn't matter what people did or didn't do in the past. It's time to explore new ways of addressing your caregiving situation. Your health and well-being depend on welcoming support from your community of friends, family, and professionals. Your collaboration directly affects the quality of care you provide your loved one. Remember that your self-care today is an investment in the rest of your life.

People have other commitments, so be considerate and gracious with people and flexible with their schedules. Recognize there are four good answers to your request for help: Yes, No, Not right now, or Maybe. Continue the conversation to explore: How would they like to help? When are they available?

Ask for what you need today:

- Can you help me prepare dinner today?

- Can you help me by researching a treatment?

- Can you help me brainstorm questions for an appointment?

- Are you available to come with me to an appointment on Monday?

- Can you help us evaluate the treatment options?

- Are you available for twenty minutes to listen while I talk things out?

Please visit www.HOCToni.com/actionplan/
for a free download of Appendix 8.

APPENDIX 9

Self-Care Action Plans

PHYSICAL

Taking care of your body, eating healthy, getting enough sleep, consistently moving or exercising your body, and paying attention to any medical needs.

1. **Nutrition—Eat healthier.** Start here. Eating nutritious food improves your health, wellness, and energy. What do you know about healthy eating? Probably a lot. You could be eating more fruits and vegetables. You may eat food that is high or excessive in carbohydrates and sugar, including processed or packaged foods. Many are allergic to dairy and haven't quit eating ice cream. How about portions? Are you reading the information provided on your packaged food? It's there for a reason. What are you snacking on, and what can be a replacement? How about eating a healthy salad for lunch? (Goodness—they come pre-packaged today in the grocery store! No excuse!)

Name and assess the validity of your excuses for not engaging in better physical self-care.

2. **Movement—Find an exercise that you enjoy.** Replace the word "exercise" with the word "movement." Movement is not formal exercise like spending an hour at the gym, though if that fits your lifestyle, keep it in your schedule. Make it as simple as

possible so it is doable. Wake up your body with 5-10 minutes of stretching in the morning. Take a break every hour and move around the house, walk outside in the fresh air for 5 minutes, or ride a stationary (or moving) bicycle for 10 minutes. Explore an online or in-person yoga class. Park a little farther from the grocery store entrance, and consider purchasing a piece of training or exercise equipment that doesn't take up a lot of space in your home. Take a break and work in your garden. Dance in your living room. Designate a "Wake-Up Song" and sing and move your body to the music.

Name and assess the validity of your excuses for not engaging in more movement.

3. **A great night's sleep—Establish a bedtime routine and what time you get up in the morning.** If lack of sleep or poor sleep quality is an issue, consider a nap during the day. If you need someone to come in and care for your loved one so you can have some downtime to rest, add that person to your Care Community™. Determine how much sleep you need to wake up in the morning feeling rested. It is probably 7 to 8 hours a night.

Name and assess the validity of your excuses for not engaging in a great night's sleep.

4. **Support your physical body.** Chiropractic, annual physical, body massage, stretching, dancing, yoga, essential oils, daily meditation, mindfulness, and journaling. What can you add? Schedule a doctor or dental appointment or wellness visit.

Name and assess the validity of your excuses for not supporting your physical body.

EMOTIONAL

Relationships that nurture, love, and support; activities that nourish you. In business, we call it networking. In our personal lives, we call it socializing and building relationships. No matter the words, your emotional well-being is essential to your quality of life and happiness.

1. Who are the people in your life who nourish and support you? Who can you talk to easily?

2. You will benefit from people who understand what you are going through as a caregiver and can empathize with or validate your experience. Seek caregiver support groups in person, a Certified Caregiver Consultant™, a caregiver chat room, or an online caregiving group.

3. Schedule activities to enjoy with a friend. It can be in person or virtual. Invite them to spend time with you and your loved one.

4. If you need to expand your friendships, can you talk to a trusted friend who may invite you and another of their friends to meet?

5. Share daily hugs and a kiss with your loved one.

6. Are there people in your life who criticize, complain, or upset you when you visit with them? What relationships consistently add to your stress? How can you gently tell them that this relationship isn't serving you? How can you shift a negative conversation?

7. Is there an unresolved conflict with a family member? Is addressing and resolving this situation best or communicating less frequently with them?

8. Perhaps there is a relationship you need to end because it hasn't served you in a long time since that person isn't kind or supportive toward you.

9. You may need more quality friendships. If you feel that your relationships are superficial, what can you do to connect with these individuals at a deeper level? Who will you call first?

10. To whom can you offer your help or support? Who can you ask for help?

11. Spend some calming time playing with your pet.

12. Learn to practice mindfulness or meditation to be aware and present in the moment. Two minutes a day can make a big difference.

13. Keep a journal. The simple act of writing things down is nourishing.

14. Connect with nature.

15. Connect with art or creativity.

16. Laugh every day. Read the comics, and listen to comedy on TV or other media.

17. Listen to your favorite music on the radio, CD, or online videos while carrying out your daily activities.

18. Treat yourself with kindness, especially when encountering challenging times.

19. Know what brings you joy.

20. Walk a friend's dog.

Name and assess the validity of your excuses for not engaging in emotional support.

MENTAL

Engage in activities that keep you sharp and alert and that you enjoy.

1. Your caregiving challenges may be your primary intellectual engagement. You may be learning about a disease, seeking information on medications, clinical trials, and surgical procedures, or looking for local resources. Books, blogs, and organizations' websites are perfect places to seek and find that information.

2. The challenge is to go beyond caregiving. Assess what your intellectual pursuits were before caregiving. Is there something you loved that has dropped out because your caregiving responsibilities absorb the time, or you cannot get away to attend activities?

3. Is there a friend who is always reading the new book and might be eager to share the information and have a conversation with you?

4. Can you spare ten minutes a day to read a book that will inspire you?

5. What do you want your life to be like when caregiving ends? Can you begin to create this vision or research possible options?

6. Connect with people over a common interest.

7. Play a musical instrument.

8. Learn something new. A game. Cards. Work a jigsaw puzzle.

9. Write in your journal.

10. Make a collage or create something artistic.

11. Listen to a podcast or take an online course.

Name and assess the validity of your excuses for not engaging in intellectual pursuits.

SPIRITUAL or RELIGIOUS

Establishing a deeper connection with your higher self or creator.

1. What are your current activities that foster your spiritual or religious involvement or development? Are you a member of a faith-based congregation? Is there a way to stay active or get support from your community? You could use their resources, guidance, retreats, reflection, and services for help. How has your faith or spiritual development changed since caregiving? Is there someone you can talk to? (See Part VII, Mistake # 20)

2. Have you read the latest book by your favorite spiritual leader? Is there an online conference you can join?

3. Have you kept a positive mindset while caregiving and focused on peace daily? Have you tried meditation or mindfulness practices? Find a space to unwind and relax. You can take 5-10 minutes to listen to calming music, practice deep breathing, meditate, or pray. Consider consistency rather than quantity of time. Download a free app onto your cell phone.

4. Who in your Care Community™ can be a resource or support for you spiritually?

5. Start a scrapbook or photo album.

6. Forgive someone. Free yourself from the burden of having been wronged.

7. Forgive yourself. Focus on the positive. Journal everything you do well and what goes right in your life. The human journey is not about perfection. It is about learning, growing, and loving.

8. Rather than berating and judging yourself harshly, compassion for yourself gives you the energy to look at options and move forward.

9. Remember, you matter. You are amazing. You are doing a fantastic job!

Name and assess the validity of your excuses for not engaging in spiritual or religious self-care.

PRACTICAL

Routines, Activities You Enjoy, Getting Organized.

1. Make a list. Any list. Get it out of your head. Write it all down.

2. Make a daily priority list and schedule your get-to-do list in your daily planner or calendar.

3. Organization. Organize a workspace, declutter a drawer, and shred unwanted mail and old paperwork.

4. Financial. Balance your checkbook, pay bills, create a budget, invest assets wisely, and list your credit cards and expenditures in a spreadsheet or notebook.

5. Plan and prepare meals for the week. Watch the specials at the grocery store, create a shopping list, and go to the store and shop.

6. Garden. Pull weeds. Buy a houseplant. Walk barefoot in the grass.

7. Visit the beach. Sit in the sun for 10 minutes. Go swimming.

Name and assess the validity of your excuses for not engaging in getting organized and having fun.

Please visit www.HOCToni.com/actionplan/
for a free download of Appendix 9.

APPENDIX 10

Do Something Fun and Uplifting (Start by coloring this list!)

- ♥ Express Love
- ♥ 30-second Hug
- ♥ Laugh
- ♥ A hot shower
- ♥ Snack on healthy food and savor the taste
- ♥ Focus on your breath for two minutes
- ♥ Send a text or an email message or a greeting card or letter in the mail
- ♥ Take a drive on a scenic road
- ♥ Ride your bike around the block
- ♥ Listen to your favorite song and music
- ♥ Dance
- ♥ Sit quietly and listen to the rain

- Wrap yourself in a warm towel just out of the dryer
- Dress up in your favorite clothes
- Make yourself a milkshake or your favorite ice cream dessert
- Call and talk with a good friend
- Enjoy a lazy bubble bath
- Read your favorite poem, book, quote, or inspiring passage
- Reminisce with your loved one
- Walk on the beach
- Walk on the grass
- Walk through your garden
- Smell the flowers
- Run through the sprinklers
- Buy yourself a small gift for under $10 or $20
- Sit in a garden and enjoy the colors and the scents
- Compliment someone
- Tell a friend what you like about them
- Meet a friend for lunch
- Listen to or watch a comedy show
- Make a new friend

- ♥ Call someone you haven't talked to in a long time

- ♥ Spend time with a friend, old or new

- ♥ Play with a puppy

- ♥ Ask someone to massage your shoulders or back

- ♥ Have a cup of hot chocolate

- ♥ Bake chocolate chip cookies and share them with friends

- ♥ Dress up for Halloween

- ♥ Attend a play or concert

- ♥ Do something today you would consider silly

- ♥ Google a fun topic to explore

- ♥ Hold hands with someone you care about

- ♥ Give someone you like an unexpected gift

- ♥ Watch the sunrise or sunset

- ♥ Give thanks for another beautiful day

- ♥ Write three Gratitudes

- ♥ Pray, meditate, or sit in silence for a bit

- ♥ Attend a social event

- ♥ Invite a friend over for lunch or to help you with a project

- ♥ Ask for help

- ♥ Smile, right now, smile

- ♥ Look at photographs or videos that inspire or improve your mood

- ♥ Write down all the good things in your life

- ♥ Write down three amazing things that happened today

- ♥ Take a nap

- ♥ Get a good night's sleep

- ♥ Move today—anything—get up and walk, jump, wiggle

Acknowledge yourself for being such an incredible and loving human.

Please visit www.HOCToni.com/actionplan/
for a free download of Appendix 10.

ACKNOWLEDGMENTS

In memory of Mom and Dad who were always there for me. My bond with Mom reached new depths throughout the years I cared for her and as she expressed her incredible love for me.

Thanks to Denise M. Brown for your caregiver consultant training program and the many opportunities you provided, including giving me the foundation and tools to begin helping family caregivers.

Thanks to my partner, Dennis, for your love, patience, support, and understanding while I wrote this book.

Thanks to Junie Swadron, Theresa Wilbanks, and Lynn Thompson for your editorial guidance and encouragement and for making writing this book a fantastically fun journey. Like caregiving, writing a book is not a solo activity, and you each brought this message to life and gave it wings.

It takes a community to write a good book. Steve Harrison, his coaching staff, and his group of authors provided education, guidance, and inspiration to keep me engaged and clear that my message is important and needs a voice.

I greatly appreciate my first readers, Dennis Dulniak, Helen Carter, and Karen Briskey.

A huge thank you to Maggie Morgan and Theresa Wilbanks for your marketing and social media expertise, and Becky Norwood, for all you and your staff accomplished to get my book published on time and with love and enthusiasm for this project.

Gratitude to all the caregivers I have met and coached. You validated over and over that this book and the information in it change lives. While the worries, mistakes, and concerns are real, you have created meaningful journeys through effective communication, asking for help, making memories, and celebrating with the loved ones in your care.

ABOUT THE AUTHOR

With 40 years in the healthcare industry, personal development training, and caring for her mom for fourteen years, Toni Gitles is an expert in teaching people to be confident, supportive caregivers. Toni navigated physical, emotional, and mental stressors, learned many lessons through trial and error, and now shares principles and practices to transform the caregiving experience into a journey of connection, advocacy, and discovery.

Caring for a family member is an act of love from the heart. However, you can lose touch with your heart connection to your care journey when the struggles and challenges outweigh the cherished moments and memories. Toni strives to keep love at the forefront by encouraging caregivers to embrace their role and thrive, helping them to avoid the pitfalls and roadblocks on the journey that may derail them from a meaningful experience.

Toni is a Certified Caregiving Consultant™, Certified Caregiving Educator™, Support Group Facilitator, Happiness Trainer, and professional speaker. Her training and personal experience enable Toni to meet family caregivers where they are, whether their loved one's health issue is due to aging or a chronic or progressive disease. Toni gently guides caregivers by offering advice, resources, and a compassionate ear.

Toni and her partner, Dennis Dulniak, locate restaurants willing to provide Dementia-friendly Dining. Additionally, owners of establishments reach out to Toni and Dennis after seeing them in the media. The pair train restaurant staff with information about dementia, situations they may encounter, and how to interact with family members and the person with dementia to create a pleasant and memorable experience for all of them. For Dementia-friendly Dining, the restaurant owner provides a quiet area and establishes specific days at off-peak times.

For more information visit:
www.centralfloridadementia-friendlydining.com/

Toni and Dennis also organize conferences with Elite Supported Travel on Holland America Cruise Lines for caregivers and their loved ones with dementia-related diseases.

For more information and to join them, visit:
www.elitecruisesandvacationstravel.com/upcoming-dementia-friendly-cruises.html

Toni's ultimate goal is to change the conversation in the United States about caregiving and people with disabilities. Medical personnel benefit by acknowledging family caregivers as knowledgeable support systems who help maintain their patient's health and well-being. All people need to be respected and understood. People who understand caregiving and common diseases that affect us encourage others to be more kind, compassionate, and helpful to families in their communities.

An international speaker who contributed to three caregiving and lifestyle management books, Toni Gitles is the author of the new book *21 Mistakes Caregivers Make & How to Avoid Them: Solutions and Strategies to Reduce Stress and Increase Happiness*, available September 2023.

Toni is a competitive ballroom dancer in her free time and enjoys gardening and playing with her Maltese dog, Jasmine. She is a volunteer with the Myasthenia Gravis Foundation of America (MGFA), and in 2022, she received the Emerging Leadership Award from the Foundation.

CONTACT TONI

YOU MAY HAVE QUESTIONS ABOUT INFORMATION IN THIS BOOK

I would love the opportunity to guide you through the potholes and emotional swings of this wild and crazy journey. Please call me. I have the experience and enough tools to lessen your burden, support you, and save you time and money. I'll be generous with my time, you will get to know me, and you will discover if working with me is something you would like to do. There is no cost to get started.

Please visit **www.heartofcaregiving.com** to schedule your no-obligation call.

Toni Gitles, CEO of Caregiver Empowerment,
Heart Light Enterprises LLC

Website: www.HeartOfCaregiving.com or www.HOCToni.com
Email: Toni@HOCTonic.om

Social Media Links
Facebook Group – Heart of Caregiving,
https://www.facebook.com/groups/568316578647069
Twitter – @HofCaregiving
https://twitter.com/HofCaregiving
Instagram – @heartofcaregiving
https://www.instagram.com/heartofcaregiving/
LinkedIn – https://www.linkedin.com/in/toni-gitles/
Linktree – https://linktr.ee/tonigitles

Please visit Amazon for your copy of the *21 Mistakes Workbook* and contact Toni for quantity discounts.

Hire Toni to Speak!

Toni is a Keynote Speaker and Workshop Facilitator

Please visit HOCToni.com/speaking/ for presentation topics and to inquire about how Toni empowers caregivers.

Transform Mistakes into Super Powers

Official companion to the book, *21 Mistakes Caregivers Make & How to Avoid Them*

Complete these action plans to avoid common mistakes, and find solutions for reducing stress, increasing happiness, and creating a meaningful caregiving journey

For individual copies, order through Amazon

For bulk orders, please contact Toni at Toni@HOCToni.com

Order the *21 Mistakes Caregivers Make & How to Avoid Them Workbook* at HOCToni.com!

Empower Caregivers

Retail $19.95 plus tax & shipping

Quantity Discounts

A special gift for the caregivers on your staff or your friends, family members, and colleagues

5-20 Books	$14.95 Each
21-50 Books	$11.95 Each
51-1,000 Books	Call for Pricing

To Place an Order
Toni Gitles
407-304-6534
Toni@HOCToni.com
or go to HOCToni.com

Heart of Caregiving